To Duncan
with love from
La Bijou xxxx
10-7-83

FORBIDDEN
Fantasies

men who dare to dress in drag

FORBIDDEN Fantasies

Photographs by
MIKE PHILLIPS
and
BARRY SHAPIRO

Text and Interviews by
MARK JOSEPH

COLLIER BOOKS
A Division of Macmillan Publishing Co., Inc.
New York
COLLIER MACMILLAN PUBLISHERS
London

Book design: Gary Nichamin/Boom! Graphics

All original black and white photographs were
printed on Ilford Galerie paper.

Macmillan Publishing Co., Inc.
866 Third Avenue, New York, N.Y. 10022
Collier Macmillan Canada, Ltd.

Library of Congress Cataloging in Publication Data
Phillips, Mike, 1945–
    Forbidden fantasies.
    1. Homosexuals, Male—California—San Francisco.
2. Transvestism.   3. Impersonators, Female.
4. Halloween.   5. Sexual fantasies.   I. Shapiro,
Barry, 1937–, joint author.   II. Joseph, Mark,
joint author.   III. Title.
HQ76.2.U5P44   306.7′6   80-13397

ISBN 0-02-006300-8

10 9 8 7 6 5 4 3 2 1

Printed in the United States of America

Contents

Foreword

A man who dresses as a woman violates a tabu that is deeply ingrained in our culture. Even in this era of gay liberation, which is scarcely a decade old, homosexuals are expected to be discreet, to avoid flaunting their departure from convention. Since colonial times, the price for indiscretion has ranged from ostracism and the pillory to prison, the insane asylum, castration, and murder. Americans prefer the illusion that homosexuals do not exist, or, if their presence among us must be acknowledged, the illusion that they can be repressed forever. Gay Americans tend to prefer the illusions of the closet, the carefully contrived illusions that protect them from the terrors of a violently intolerant society.

Drag queens conspicuously defy the tabu. Ordinarily, they do not appear in public—the risk is too great—but remain behind closed doors at their own private parties and in their own clubs. All too often, these clubs are seedy bars in unsavory parts of town, known only to themselves, their admirers, and the police. Their very existence is a threat to the security of the tremendously varied and complex homosexual culture as a whole. The very act of crossdressing calls attention to itself and incurs the wrath of a society which reacts hysterically to any challenge by nonconformists. As a result of repression, drag queens have remained a mystery, living within their own carefully concealed, indeed forbidden, world.

Once a year, on Halloween, this world bursts forth into the open. On Halloween, costuming is sanctioned, and what has remained hidden all year walks flamboyantly out into the streets. This ancient pagan autumn festival, adopted centuries ago by Christians as Allhallows' Eve and in the last century by children as a night of trick or treat, has become the gay national holiday.

In the city of San Francisco, which in the last few years has become known as "the gay capital of the world," Halloween is celebrated as a gigantic festival that draws hundreds of thousands into the streets. The festivities center around Polk and Castro streets, the main thoroughfares of two predominately gay neighborhoods. The streets are closed to traffic, bands play, tourists gawk, the queens parade, intoxicants of every description are consumed in vast quantities, and everyone has one hell of a party. Unfortunately, it is not always in good fun. In recent years, the celebrants have been mightily harassed by roving gangs of teenage thugs who attempt to turn the party into a riot.

Our original intention was to document Halloween, to photograph the amazing array of costumes that appear in the streets during the one legitimate masquerade in our calendar. To this end we photographed one hundred twenty-five people, which resulted in one thousand color transparencies and one overwhelming question: Who are these people?

As three non-gay men, we knew nothing about drag queens, but we did know we had captured something special and unique. The queens had all retreated into their private world, and the only way to find out who they were was to go in after them and inquire of them directly.

The search took a year and led us to every part of San Francisco: to the gay bars on Castro Street, the sidewalks of Polk Street, the leather bars, the drag clubs, the Tenderloin, the ghetto, the middle-class suburbs. As each interview progressed, a stereotype peeled away, new questions were raised, old answers failed. We found full-time queens, part-time queens, one-time queens, and people who were not queens at all. Most, but not all, of the people we photographed and interviewed are gay. A few were born and raised in the San Francisco Bay Area, but the majority, like most San Franciscans, come from every part of the United States. They vary in age from eighteen to thirty-four, in attitude from totally spaced out to very conservative, in occupation from professional female impersonator to high school teacher.

As Michael, the Lady in Pink, says in the first interview, they will make you "open your eyes real big."

MARK JOSEPH
MIKE PHILLIPS
BARRY SHAPIRO

Acknowledgments

A work of this scope would not have been possible without the encouragement and support of many people. The authors would like to thank: Howard Brainen of Custom Process, Berkeley, Maggi Britt, Victoria Butler, Bob Dattila, Joel Huckins, Sharon Jacobs, John McDermott, Ernie Merriweather, Bill Poplar, Nancy Rosenblum, Helen Shapiro, Susan Sherry Shapiro, Ed Tenny, Dan Turk, and a very special thanks to Jon Korchin for his photographic assistance on Halloween.

1. The Lady in Pink

MICHAEL

All day Michael stands behind the counter of a fashionable cafeteria in the ultramodern Embarcadero Center and serves up soup. Subtly adorned with the badges of his sexuality—a hard rubber cockring on his wrist, a neatly folded red handkerchief in the right hip pocket of his Levis—he ladles up chicken gumbo today, split pea tomorrow, idly dreaming the afternoon away. The well-dressed downtown noontime crowd stretches before him, an endless line of polyester flesh.

He eyeballs them all, waiting for a signal, a wink, or brazen flirtation that unleashes the dazzling smile.

Michael comes from Milpitas, a San Francisco suburb dominated by a massive Ford assembly plant. Most of the citizens of Milpitas are as indistinguishable from one another as the cars that come off the assembly line, but occasionally the town, like Ford, will turn out something unique, a prototype, a customized version of a human being.

After work, Michael parties, and we

partied with him. We accompanied him to The Stud, a cavernous bar on Folsom Street's "Chain Lane," packed with hundreds of sweating, boisterous men. With its young crowd, The Stud has probably witnessed more coming-out parties than the cotillion ballroom of the Palace Hotel.

Within five minutes after entering The Stud, Michael was sequestered in a corner with an instant lover. Fifteen minutes later they parted and he found another. The disco music was so loud it was impossible to hear a spoken word, but no one goes to The Stud to converse.

In or out of drag, Michael is a stopper. His androgynous beauty dominates any scene, but he is totally without arrogance. People like to look at Michael, to touch and pet him. Still growing up in the era of gay liberation, Michael's wonderful, childlike innocence has not been distorted by the rigors of repression.

How did you plan your Halloween costume, Michael?

Well, it's always the same, always a show-girl. I always make it look sexy 'cause the boys get off on that. It was just something I felt comfortable with, and, you know, gave them a show. I like to entertain.

Did you go out by yourself?

Uh-huh. See, my roommate was working and my other friend, well, he wasn't ready and he didn't really want to go, and I had everything planned, what I was going to wear and all that stuff, so I said, "Go on, Michael, go by yourself. You're a big boy. Do it." So I did.

Tell us about the very first time you went in drag.

That was a Halloween party for my sixteenth birthday. I wore one of my sister's dresses, this Hawaiian print dress that was strapless and real colorful, and my mother's black wig, and I threw on makeup, not real good, just on my lips and eyes, and I told my mother I was going in drag.

Well, I was standing at the door and my mother was talking to this guy and he kept looking at me and looking at me and finally he said, "Who is that pretty girl?" and my mother said, "Buckley, that's my son."

Oh, he was just really wrecked. That was the only time I did it 'til I moved into the city three years ago. It was like, you know, things just happened automatically and so I just got into it, just by making all these people open their eyes real big.

Open their eyes to what?

Just to see something like me. On Hallow-een there was a point when I would just stand and they would crowd around

me and just stare. I mean they would look at every detail. And I just did it 'cause when you do it you got to do it good, 'cause these queens talk, uh-huh, they talk good, and I thought I did everything right and I would stand there and they would look at me from head to toe and they were just amazed. I loved it. It was hot.

THAT BRACELET. IS THAT A COCKRING? IT LOOKS PRETTY BIG...
It is. It's mine and it fits. Most straight people don't know what it is, but some of them can guess. Sometimes when people come through the line and I serve them they ask questions that don't ever need to be asked. Just dumb, real dumb. Every person who comes through the line is the same...thousands...you'd think they'd catch on but they don't.

Once I had a button—it was me in drag—I did this green sailor's uniform and this curly wig and I had this hat on. I looked just like Alice, that waitress at Bud's Diner on TV, and, anyway, somebody took a picture and we cut it up and made a button and I wore it to work. A lot of people looked but didn't say anything. Some of the men know but most, they don't know. See, here in the Embarcadero Center people don't experience things like that.

WHAT DO YOU LIKE BEST IN LIFE, MICHAEL?
Going to parties and going to the discos. Having fun. One night I was real loaded and I wanted to write a book about me, just about me growing up fast in the city, because I graduated and I left the next day and I've been here ever since and, boy, I learned a lot. I did. I learned just a whole bunch of things. 'Cause, see, in school I learned how to read and write and how to add and subtract and how to dissect a frog, things like that that you need to know to get by. In the city you gotta work hard, have a real good job, and work at your job. If a man would go to bed and he would get up, he would always be on time to work.

YOU MANAGE TO PARTY 'TIL ALL HOURS AND STILL GET TO WORK ON TIME...
Well, I'm strong. I've been late maybe three times, but it was my own fault like everybody else. I've had a job and I've had a nice, a real good life. I'm happy. I don't make lots of money but I'm still happy. This is my third job in the city. I was working at one place and they got real pissed off. I dunno, they just said they didn't like me the way I was. They said, "You just wouldn't fit in anymore for our restaurant." And, you know, it was like, that ain't no excuse! But I'm saving up my money now and I'm going to move to New York. I want to model clothes.

MEN'S CLOTHES OR WOMEN'S CLOTHES?
Men's like *GQ*. That woman trip is only at night. It's like a fantasy.

IT GETS TIRESOME AFTER A WHILE, GOING TO WORK AND THEN GOING TO THE DISCO, THEN GETTING UP AND GOING BACK TO WORK...
Yup! That's exactly the time to move on. I want to see more. Like, who does all this creation? There's thousands of people making all these clothes, but how do they know what styles to make next month? I wonder how do people get all this knowledge to make all this. God, it took a lot of work to build this building and, where are all the plans? You can watch 'em building bars and bars and bars and all of a sudden you see all this creation. Whoever thought of that? It's amazing, all the detail work. In school you would go on a field trip, say you went to a chocolate-chip factory and you would see how chocolate-chip cookies are made. You know, a lot of people don't experience all this stuff on how things are processed. They don't know about the thousands of people who work in the chocolate-chip factory. I wonder about all that. Yeah!

2. The Stripper

A drag queen, like an actress, creates a deliberate illusion with clothes, makeup, and attitude. The fewer illusions he has about himself, the better he knows himself, the more successful the illusion will be. The most successful queens make a quantum leap to self-realization, and thus transcend the limited, visible reality to reveal an inner, more profound truth.

When Chuckie started doing public drag on the hostile streets of Milwaukee, Wisconsin, before the days of

CHUCKIE

gay liberation, any illusions he might have had were beaten out of him. Yet the more the public and its agents, the police, the media, and the courts, tried to suppress him, the more adamantly he proclaimed his right to self-expression.

For years he has endured the sometimes harsh existence of a struggling music writer, composing songs on an old piano, and drawing on a huge six-by-ten easel. He lives alone in a loft space, part of a vast artists' commune in a converted

warehouse, with his irrepressible dog Zoomer, who contrived to get into almost every photograph.

WHAT KIND OF MUSIC DO YOU WRITE, CHUCKIE?
Well, my friend Mina calls them torchy ballads.

HOW LONG HAVE YOU BEEN AT IT?
Years and years.

HAVE YOU HAD ANY SUCCESS?
No, I've been much more successful as a drag queen than as a musician.

WHEN DID YOU START GOING INTENSELY INTO DRAG?
Well, I used to work with a group in Los Angeles called The Bonbons, which was originally from Milwaukee, Wisconsin. We got a lot of publicity and we hit in various magazines and things.

The Bonbons encompassed all types of people and when you have that many people with different interests it's hard to sustain a focus. I wanted to focus somewhere and someone else wanted to focus somewhere else and that led to the natural demise. When we moved the operation to Los Angeles we were invited to a lot of places because we were known for what we were doing, and it added something to your party to have us, but The Bonbons weren't interested in doing anything commercial, like having anything marketable, which is why, basically, it burned itself out.

DO YOU SEE DRAG AS AN ART FORM OR AS AN EXPRESSION OF YOUR SEXUALITY?

It's both, really. I think it definitely is an art form and it really takes a talent. We're always trying to think up new drags, new ways to create illusions. When you're doing female impersonation, you try to pass as much as you decide you want to pass, with the obvious aim that you're trying to portray something. Sometimes you're dressing up just to dress up, doing something that looks good, something flashier. Then you're not trying to pass off any illusion that you're a woman, you're just trying to pass off that you're dressed up.

HOW OLD WERE YOU WHEN YOU FIRST WENT IN DRAG?

I was four, I think. The first memory I have of anything is of being in drag. I've gone in drag all of my life. My dress-up clothes were always dresses, a whole stock of dresses and things like that. I had a pair of stunning red straw high heels that I wore to kindergarten and first grade, but after that I don't remember going to school in drag except on Halloween. Almost every Halloween I've ever spent I've gone in some kind of drag.

THE BONBONS?

The Bonbons started as a group of arty-type drag queens, basically all drag queens who were involved in art somewhere else along the line and were sort of tired of where they were and what they were doing and simply decided to *do* something. With the everyday drag that everyone was doing, it was obvious that it would be more successful as a group, and so we just did it and played it to where it would go. We made it into a life-art kind of thing and so people took it more as art than as drag, but all the while it was just basically drag.

On Halloween I like to do something that's more costumish than I normally would. I don't like to go in drag on Halloween just to go in drag. I like to have some kind of theme under it, so if I go in drag I'm going in drag as something. This year I was a stripper. If it's not a theme-type drag, like on Halloween, I usually try to look as I would if I were really a woman. If I were really a woman, what would I be doing? I usually try to do secretaries.

Do you feel as though you are a woman?

No, but I'm not uncomfortable being a woman. I think going in drag is fine. I think men's clothes are basically boring to be done all the time, and I think everybody is naturally drawn to things that are more flamboyant. I'm not hesitant at all to identify as a woman or be identified as a woman, and I don't have the inhibitions to stop myself from wanting to do that. I think that most people's inhibitions about drag come from their attitude towards women. It's not their attitude about being gay, obviously, because not all transvestites are gay. Even serious, everyday transvestites are not always gay, but many gay men have feelings that women are shit. There's all different kinds of gay men and all different kinds of drag queens, and lots and lots of straight men who are interested in drag queens.

A few years ago conditions for drag queens were much less fun, but recently I've noticed attitudes are changing. People are much more receptive. I get many more propositions when I'm in drag than not in drag, but there are some people that just don't like it. It was tabu for a while, but the times are changing.

Do you think there will be an anti-gay backlash?

To me it doesn't matter. I've lived through pretty much the worst that could happen. I lived in *Milwaukee*, I mean pre-gay liberation when there was nothing to protect anybody. You were beaten on the street and people would stop and help the beaters instead of the victim.

Did that happen to you?

Oh, God, yeah, many times. When I was younger I was out on the street in forms of drag and got into lots of trouble. It used to happen anywhere at any time, in the middle of shopping centers, wherever. It was sanctioned so unless they absolutely allow people to walk the streets with guns with bullets marked for faggots, I don't see how it could be worse. I didn't grow up being gay after the time of gay liberation, I did it before. The police were still raiding bars and that kind of thing. I'm used to it. It could happen again and it might be bad but I think I'd make it through, again.

When I was eighteen, a friend of mine and I went into a television station in Milwaukee and made an hour and a half tape, which they cut to five minutes and put on the news every night with our names in big white letters. All of a sudden I was notorious. Gay lib was just starting to happen and I immediately went on this gay lib crusade where I was doing TV and radio and getting in the papers all the time. My parents were embarrassed and I moved out of the house. I would apply for jobs and people would openly laugh at me and there wasn't any kind of recourse. It was *allowed* to be discriminatory.

When we were doing gay liberation we got involved in all the other causes we thought were worth supporting. We demonstrated against Spiro Agnew and Kent State, and we were the gay contingent at the first May Day march on

Washington, D.C. You've got to remember that when all this happened we not only didn't have the support of straight people, but we didn't have the support of many gay people either. They thought we were really crazy radicals. It got to the point where everywhere I went there was a confrontation either with somebody straight or somebody gay, and I just didn't want to be involved anymore.

After a year and a half, I got caught stealing a car. It was real strange. I was arrested with these two straight men and I didn't know them very well, and we happened to be arrested in my hometown, a suburb of Milwaukee. We were returning from the Black Panther Convention in Philadelphia and I had on a bright yellow gay-lib shirt with huge red symbols, and big earrings and black fingernails, and I was just stunning. The police didn't like that. In jail

they gave the two straight men breakfast but didn't give me anything. I went to court every day in drag and the judge didn't like me and the bailiffs would say things and I would say things back. On sentencing I was in drag, and the judge asked me why I didn't have a job, and I said I thought it was because I was gay, and he asked, "What is that?" and I said, "Well, that's homosexual," and he just turned and said, "Well, maybe the reason you can't get a job is because of the way you dress, and I hereby order you to see a psychiatrist."

There's always this shit going on. I've had it all along, all along.

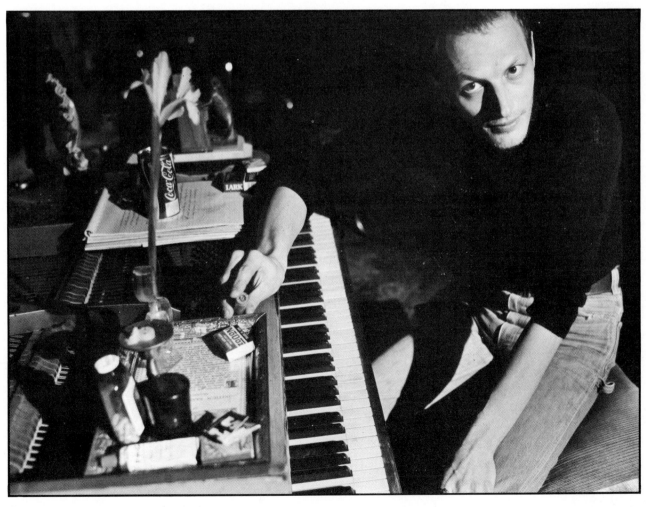

3. Donna Mae Roz

The Hotel Zee, rooms $35 a week with bath, $25 without. No visitors after ten P.M. A sign in the lobby says, "No dope smoking in the elevator or front lounge." This is the Tenderloin, the soft tissue of the inner city, the well-marbled meat of the Barbary Coast. On every block the odor of sex and drugs permeates the porno shops, the cheap hotels, the sinister, dark taverns: The Trapp, The Roadrunner, The Peter Pan. Here, life is cheap, like white port and Quaaludes. In the pawnshop windows, trinkets glitter like broken dreams of California gold.

DONALD

Donald, twenty years old, alone and broke, fluttered about his $35 room on a Wednesday night fretting about his rent due the next morning. Only a few months before, he was playing high-school football in Cedar Rapids, Iowa, and his sleek athlete's body seemed out of place against the cracked walls and chipped paint.

YOU WERE A FOOTBALL PLAYER?
Oh, yeah. I was a *jock*!

WHAT POSITION?
First-string defensive tackle and second-string fullback.
SO YOU WENT BOTH WAYS...
Yeah. *(Laughs)* I never thought of it that way. I loved it. I played football for five years and ran track and did wrestling.
DO YOU STILL LIKE TO WORK OUT?
Only when I'm pushed into it. Sometimes at the gym, see, there are a lot of guys who love gay men, they just don't like drag queens in the sense that what they want to get away from is women, then this man dressed up as a woman shows up and just turns them off. So I get rejected a whole lot because I drag. But also, the compliments and stuff make up for it.
HOW LONG HAVE YOU BEEN GOING IN DRAG?
A few weeks.

There's a lot of drag queens that live here at the hotel, and I'm not that macho butch of a man and I wanted to try it, so I tried it. It was just like a different world. People were opening up doors for me, buying me drinks, telling me how good I looked and everything. It was a big ego trip. Whenever I get down and depressed I hop in drag.
IS YOUR FAMILY AWARE OF YOUR LIFE-STYLE?
To a degree. They don't know I wear women's clothes but they know I'm gay. They found out this summer and it was really weird. I came in at like six o'clock in the morning in drag, and it was really tacky drag, hot pants and five-inch pumps and my hair wrapped up with chopsticks in it, so I was like a seven-foot-two

woman. I was with this man and I had all these drag pictures and naked men up on the wall, and my room looked kinda gay, and somebody knocked on the door while we were in bed, and said, "Donnie, your mom's here." I said, "Go away," because I knew she wasn't there; she teaches on an air force base in Germany. "But she *is* here," he said, so I tiptoed down the back stairway and there was my mom sitting in the lobby. Panic! Panty-hose, women's shoes, pictures torn off the wall. Oh! It was terrible, dresses and hose and coats and makeup. But then I went shopping with my mom and I told her I was gay, and, um, she's real religious, and that made it worse, 'cause, um, it's a sin to lie in bed with another man. She told me all of this and she gave me a gold Bible, and decided that no matter what, she was always going to love me. I thought that was neat.

I told her on a Friday, and on Saturday morning my dad was here. They're divorced and he lives in Iowa and she called him and said, "Check out your son and see what kind of trouble he's into." But Daddy said he'd known for years. I remember him taking me shopping for Christmas and I'd pick up Barbie Dolls and other dolls and he would buy 'em for me. He was very realistic and said I was to be careful because society was not as accepting toward it as he was.

WHEN DID YOU DECIDE THAT YOU WERE GAY, DONALD?
It was about a year ago. I was always saying that I was "bi," and I never came out and said I was gay, totally gay, but I was in this fraternity and one of the guys in the fraternity took me to a gay bar. Oh, I was scared to death, but we went into the bar and it was a rush seein' the men kissin' on each other, you know, and dancin' with each other and stuff. I wasn't ready for it then. I wasn't really convinced I was gay. I was more scared of it than anything else, but I kept on going to the bar and meeting people and seeing people I graduated with and the guys I played football with and I started loosening up.

AND CAME TO SAN FRANCISCO...?
Yes. San Francisco is known all over as the gay capital of the world. I thought I would have some chances here, some openings. I want to be a dancer; that's my dream, to be a dancer. I'm glad I came here but I'm disappointed in the sense that I expected things to be handed to me on a silver platter, but it just doesn't happen. If you want something bad enough you have to go out and get it. All I've been doing is just partying. I haven't taken care of business like I should have been doing. If I don't get a job I think I might have to go back home and that's a bummer.

I have friends with books of numbers that they call if they need money. They go and do tricks for thirty or forty dollars. I've tried that but I'm just not the type. I've had a lot of opportunities but I just can't do it. I went up on the 'ho' stroll in drag, and it was so neat 'cause cars were stoppin' and waitin', four cars in a line, and I'd go to one car and he'd be ooooh soooo ugly, and I'd go to the next car and he wouldn't be cute enough.

THEY'RE SUPPOSED TO PICK YOU.
I know. That's why I can't do it. If I'm
going to share something like that, it's real
personal to me, you know, sex. I want
somebody halfway decent.

HOW DID YOU CHOOSE YOUR HALLOWEEN
COSTUME?
Well, I didn't have any money so I went to
the plasma center and sold some blood
and got some money. I already had most
of the makeup and somebody gave me a
bikini so all I had to buy was the
Christmas tinsel.

IF YOU COULD BE REBORN, WOULD IT BE AS A
GAY MAN OR A WOMAN?
A woman. The only problem I have now
is that I'm so big and everything. It's so
shocking that I can get over, bein' as big
as I am, because I have big calves and
broad shoulders.

WOULD YOU LIKE TO FIND SOMEONE WITH
WHOM YOU COULD LIVE FOREVER AND EVER?
Oh, yes, of course. I want someone I could
do everything for, cook dinner, clean up the
house, pick up after him, things like that.

WOMEN DON'T FEEL THAT WAY ANYMORE.
No, they don't. But I feel I'm prettier as a
girl than as a boy, don't you?

4. Star Whores

When drag is done with talent and skill, it approaches art. When it is seen by both performers and observers as an examination of role-playing, it becomes political art. Drag is also fun.

Jersey and Felix have more fun with drag than almost anyone. Their drags are usually thematic, highly designed, and meticulously executed. Both are commercial artists with advanced training in their fields, and accustomed to thinking in terms of conceptual art. Felix is an interior

JERSEY AND FELIX

designer and Jersey an architectural illustrator.

JERSEY
WHAT DID YOU AND FELIX CALL YOURSELVES ON HALLOWEEN?
Well, the general theme for the Beaux Arts Ball, the weekend before Halloween, was movies, Hollywood movies and things like that, and we wanted to do something "space" so our movie was *Star Wars*. Felix was Della Vader, Darth's evil little sister, and my name was Starlene Starfucker, and we called ourselves star whores. My

boyfriend at the time was doing male drag, a little space cadet called Luke Starfucker, and I was supposed to be his big sister.

We went to the Ball, and most of the people were doing drag numbers but they were very serious about it. They spend most of the year and God knows how many thousands of dollars on very elaborate costumes. What we're doing is completely the opposite. We're into it for a kind of sleazy type of effect. Every time we get into drag it's always a trashy whore, sleaze-type drag, as opposed to something very elegant, movie-starish kind of thing.

WHY IS THAT?
It gives us something we can have fun with. We don't ever want to get so serious, so wrapped up in this drag costume thing that we can never pull it off. We do these things as a joke on ourselves and a joke on society and the community that we're living in. We all grew up with this kind of macho role that we're all supposed to fit into, and when we came out, of course, we realized we didn't have to fit into that role if we didn't want to. However, out of the frying pan and into the fire! We found out that many people who are gay, openly homosexual, are more serious about these macho roles than the people we just left! I'm not into doing something that's totally contrary. I wear a shirt and pants to work every day, but every once in a while it's

nice to be able to laugh at myself and the roles we're constantly doing, and to get other people to laugh at it and to loosen their feelings. Jiggle some nuts loose, I guess.

DO YOU GO IN DRAG OFTEN?
No, not often enough. It's fun. I get off on doing things a lot of people wouldn't consider doing. I get off on being outrageous, and that takes many forms. Once Felix and I went to a party at a gym and everybody who attended was doing muscles. Of course, we couldn't compete with that kind of artillery so we did the opposite and went in drag. That was the first time I ever dressed in drag.

SO YOU NEVER DRESSED UP AS A KID...
No. I never even considered it. It never dawned on me that I was capable of that kind of outrageousness. I probably suppressed it a lot, but now that I'm older and freer I can go about expressing those kinds of things.

I HEAR THE WORD "OUTRAGEOUS" ALL THE TIME. IT'S BECOME SUCH A CATCH-ALL WORD I'M NOT SURE WHAT ANYONE MEANS BY IT. YOU DON'T MEAN YOU WISH TO PROVOKE RAGE BY BEING "OUTRAGEOUS," DO YOU?
No, but you're trying to provoke some sort of emotion and in our case it's more of a happy emotion or something we can laugh at as opposed to something to throw fists at. But the reality is that dressed that way, or being outrageous in that particular way, we can provoke fists.

WHY IS THAT?
A lot of insecurity. I think people who are able to do that pose a threat to those who can't...can't bring themselves to act out the roles that they would prefer to act out, and that frustrates them to the point of violence. It doesn't necessarily have to be a drag queen. It could be a straight person who leads a particular life-style. It's a very individual thing. Maybe somebody who was brought up to be a sissy will want to become a macho man and vice versa. Everybody's trying to run away from something and find something else. The people who suffer from lack of imagination are always

going to be victims of what the media pour down their throats. For the hour or two that I'm dressed up I just want to show that it can be fun to take on other roles, anything you want to do, as long as you don't become obsessed with one role or another or infringe on somebody else's territory. I show how much fun I'm having to anyone willing to watch me.

WHAT'S YOUR NEXT ROLE?
I might do a boy drag next time. The act of dressing up or acting out or whatever you want to call it can take many forms. A boy drag would be fun, something skimpy, I guess, anything but a girl's suit that I have to wrap myself up in and can't get out of. Anything I put on for a costume on Halloween or a masquerade has to be something I can get out of easily.

YOU WANNA JUMP AROUND NAKED?
Yeah. And something I can run away in.

DID YOU TAKE IT OFF THIS HALLOWEEN?
I didn't take it off at all. Everybody wanted me to keep it on so I kept it on. See, my tits were made out of two stockings full of birdseed, I think there was a pound and a half of birdseed in each one, and through the evening that was quite a load on my shoulders, and I had a hairband in my hair that kept pulling in the opposite direction from my breasts. It was pulling up and my breasts were pulling down and I had a terrible headache. I remember walking home and taking those tits and fuh-linging them to hell. I don't know where those things landed but I hope the birds got to them.

FELIX

WHAT DO YOU DO IN THE REAL WORLD, FELIX?
The *real* world? I'm an interior designer in an architectural firm in San Francisco. We do hospitals and health-care facilities.

EVERY TIME HOLLYWOOD WANTS TO TAKE A CHEAP SHOT AT HOMOSEXUALS THEY MAKE SOME FRUITY LITTLE FAG PLAY AN INTERIOR DESIGNER...
I know. Next year for the Gay Parade I might do a stereotype interior designer with a purple suit, white glasses, pink scarf, and a lot of silk and carrying on.

WHERE ARE YOU FROM?
I grew up in Las Vegas where I got my aesthetic, but I've been in the Bay Area eleven years.

TELL US A LITTLE ABOUT YOUR HALLOWEEN
COSTUME.
My Della Rae Vader costume? Darth's evil
little sister?

YEAH. WHAT'S IT MADE OF?
Not…too…much! A wee bit, less than a
yard, of gold lamé. It's mostly hair and
two guns.

WAS "STAR WHORES" YOUR IDEA?
I can't remember where the seed of the
idea came from, but I certainly pushed it
further, to reality.

PUSH THINGS A LITTLE BIT FURTHER?…

Well, it's sort of like a gay thing to take a
straight ideal like *Star Wars* and just push
it over towards bad taste and humor.

WHEN DID YOU START DOING DRAG?
Most of my drag comes from the Cockette
days, lots of glitter on the eyes and mostly
bein' a goof. It's not like a traditional
Fifties drag queen.

TELL US ABOUT THE COCKETTES.
The Cockettes were a very loosely struc-
tured theater group that started doing
small shows around 1971. I knew some
of The Cockettes and it was a whole

political awakening. It was an awareness of what the male-female roles and types meant to people, and playing with those roles was like a freedom. It was also a lot of fun. The boys all had beards and mustaches and at that time everyone had long hair. They did all kinds of raunchy stories, all sort of sexual.

I remember the first show I saw was *The Pearls of Shanghai*, that premiered in an alley in Chinatown. There was this big chorus that was shouting, "Shanghai, Shanghai," and all the Chinese were hanging over their balconies screaming at them. I just loved it. Later they moved into a theater and had midnight shows. One night Truman Capote and Rex Reed were recognized in the audience and they were showered with joints, just joints fell from the sky. The shows were always real elaborate and just glitter for days. That's where the glitter comes from.

WHAT DISTINGUISHED THE COCKETTES FROM OTHER PEOPLE DOING DRAG AT THAT TIME?
Well, most of the time they didn't wear underwear. Their dicks were always hanging out. They never shaved their beards and it was real loose kinda hippy acid drag as opposed to a kind of Fifties glamour drag queen who was trying to be like a real woman.

WERE THE COCKETTES THE FIRST DRAG QUEENS NOT TRYING TO PASS?
Right. As far as I know. It was called the gender-fuck, which means you have elements of both sexes, either in your dress or makeup, and then you have the beard or mustache and a kind of gender mix-up,

and it comes out unique. It makes a statement and I enjoy making that statement.

AND WHAT IS THAT STATEMENT?
That it doesn't matter what you have on, it's the person behind the clothes. It's like men's liberation, liberating a man from the stereotypical male clothing and ways of reacting. A man can be effeminate and still be a man, and that was a great lesson to me. It's not that heavy of a political statement. You couldn't base a political platform on it.

ARE DRAG QUEENS OUTLAWS IN THE GAY SCENE, BEING FARTHER OUT THERE THAN ANYBODY ELSE?
Certainly, they're the most visible. It is a kind of visual rebellion. There is the feeling among people who do drag that they are walking the end of the line, the edge of society. There is a definite thrill. When I get up in drag I feel like I'm at the edge there.

IT STRIKES ME AS BEING A HELL'S ANGELS SORT OF THING...
Oh, definitely. People who see you have a very strong reaction. Hell's Angels scare the shit out of you, but drag queens really threaten or can threaten a man's whole identity of himself and idea of what a man is. It's real strong stuff.

5. Mister Christine

On Turk Street between Taylor and Jones, in the heart of the Tenderloin, whores of every sex patrol day and night. Old winos live like derelict squirrels in empty lots, while the slightly more fortunate, less addicted elderly stare across hotel lobbies transformed into geriatric wards.

In the middle of the block the faded marquee of The Sound of Music Theatre Lounge throws scant illumination on the squalid

TEDDY

scene. It is easy to mistake the little club for just another Tenderloin bar. The letters on the marquee are broken and poorly aligned, but the message they spell out—SHOWS NITELY, FEMALE IMPERSONATORS—is clear to anyone who looks.

Inside there is linoleum on the floor, plaster on the walls, and unvarnished Budweisers on the bar. Mismatched tables line either side of a narrow runway that extends from a low stage at the

back of the room. There is no curtain, only
a makeshift screen, festooned with Christmas
tinsel, separating the stage from the dressing
room. The Sound of Music is a hardcore
drag club patronized by serious queens and
their admirers—not at all like the famous
Finnochio's up on Broadway where tourists
pretend to have a risqué evening while
shuffling from tourbuses to cushioned
theater seats. There is no intellectualizing
about role-playing in The Sound of Music,
no philosophizing about drag as art; there
is only drag, pushed to the limit.

Teddy works here three nights a week, two shows a night. His act, like the others, consists of improvised dancing while he lip-synchs the lyrics to a variety of recorded music, mostly show tunes and the current disco hits. The performers appear one at a time, bounce around the stage, down the runway, and out among the tables, while the spotlight operator tries frantically to follow their erratic movements. Patrons who like a particular performer can approach him at any moment and present him with a dollar bill. At the end of the night these tips hopefully add up to quite a bit more than the minimal salary paid by the club, most of which goes for the elaborate costumes. Here, at the very core of the drag world, style and form are everything. Substance and content mean nothing.

Like most of the other entertainers, Teddy prefers classic glamour drag. His dresses are long and flowing; his makeup is immaculate; the illusion total. When he appears onstage as Mister Christine, Teddy vanishes completely.

Teddy was unnervingly elusive. On Halloween we had no idea the sexy imp in *Rocky Horror Picture Show* drag was a pro. He left us the address and phone number of a notoriously sleazy rooming house, and when we showed up for our first appointment he had vanished. The manager told us he thought Teddy was in jail and that he worked at The Sound of Music. We started hanging around the club every night until he showed up in drag as part of the audience. He was too vague and flighty to talk to us that night, but said we could meet him the following night at his new rooming house. He missed that appointment, having forgotten what day it was, but we went back the next night and caught him at home a few minutes before he went to work. We drove him to the club and interviewed him backstage while he changed his clothes, changed his face, and changed his name.

Teddy doesn't talk very much. He doesn't have to. He makes his statement simply by being Mister Christine.

WE HEARD YOU WERE IN JAIL, TEDDY. WHAT HAPPENED?
Well, I got, you know, I was out wanderin' around, fuckin' around, you know, and the vice squad picked me up and took me to jail for prostitution. It was entrapment. I knew it was but, you know, I don't want to make nothin' big out of it.

HAS THIS EVER HAPPENED TO YOU BEFORE?
It happened once before, in Dallas, but, you know, you go through these things.

WHY DID YOU COME TO SAN FRANCISCO?
Um, it's different, you know. Most guys join the service, join the navy to travel but I travel on my own. I love San Francisco. I've been here eight months but I feel like I've been here all my life.

ARE YOU GOING TO STAY?
Probably not. I'll probably move on in a year or so. I wanna go to L.A.

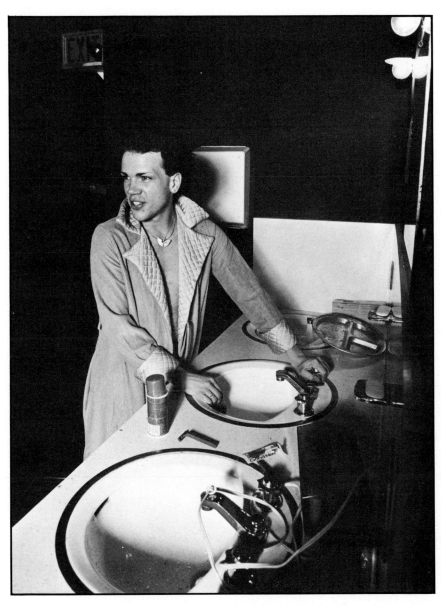

How long have you been working here at the Sound of Music?
Three weeks.
Is this the first place you've worked as an impersonator?
No, I worked at a club in Dallas and before that in Kansas City.
Tell me about the first time you dressed in drag.
The first time? Um, I was about twelve years old and I was messin' around with my sister, you know, and she had a Brownie dress so I tried it and that's what started it all.
And have you been dressing in drag ever since?
Um, since I got older, I take drag more serious now, you know. It's no fun at all. It's a lot of work.
How would you describe your halloween costume?
Outrageous.
Outrageous, hmm. were we seeing you as Christine?
No, I was trying to copy the *Rocky Horror Picture Show* trip.

At this point the stage manager of The Sound of Music interrupted the interview with, "All right, showtime. You'll have to take your interview somewhere else." We left Teddy in the dressing room, wiping away shaving cream and starting on his makeup. When we saw him a few minutes later on stage, under layers of pink chiffon, he was totally transformed into the bewitching Mister Christine.

6. Loretta

"I've always been Loretta," said Larry between sips of Jack Daniel's, "always, always, always."

It took the better part of a half-pint of bourbon to get Larry started, but then he gushed and told us the story of his life.

Just out of high school in Youngstown, Ohio, he joined the army, and when his hitch was up, he joined the navy. "I was both a WAC and a WAVE, defending our nation."

After the military, he returned to

LARRY

Ohio for four years of nursing school. "I was an outrageous faggot on campus, with a lot of star status. If you're an open gay person, a lot of people take notice."

To support himself in school he worked nights as a waiter, so when he came to San Francisco and couldn't find work as a nurse, he looked for a waitering position. On sheer panache he landed a job at the elegant Garden Court of the Sheraton-Palace Hotel and worked there a year before returning to

nursing.

A charter member of The Gay Freedom Day Marching Band and Twirling Corps, Larry plays tenor sax and sings in the chorus.

In the service, at the hotel, in a hospital, or on the parade ground with the band, Larry almost always wears a uniform, each a kind of drag that allows him to *perform*. "All my life, people have been saying, 'Go on stage, child, go on stage.' When I put on a uniform, I *am* on stage. I have a role to play. Besides, I don't have to buy clothes which are so damn expensive these days."

TELL US ABOUT YOUR HALLOWEEN, LARRY. Well, this was my first Halloween in San Francisco, so I was wondering what it would be like. I heard there was a big spectacle on Polk Street and tourists would be there, and they wanted to come down and get entertained and see some of the San Francisco freaks do it. Well, I decided that I would simply go out there and do it. I did a combination of Divine and the *Rocky Horror Picture Show*, and I had the chance to rear back and strut and be totally outrageous. If I stopped, within fifteen seconds there'd be a circle of people around me with all their flashbulbs goin'. I was strikin' and carryin' on. I would lay down in the street and this couple would come up to me and she would say, "Would you take a picture with my husband?" and I would sort of sleaze up to that person, hold him or something like that, strike a little pose. Well, they loved that type of activity.

HAVE YOU ALWAYS BEEN OPENLY GAY? Well, actually, prekindergarten I was sexually active. I didn't deal with kindergarten people at the time, of course. They didn't have a grip on sexuality. It was older people.

How old were they?
Oh, I don't know. When you're four or five years old you don't have a grip on people's ages. You just get a grip on hard things. In high school, most of the people knew I was gay. It wasn't a matter of always talking about being gay, but if someone asked me if I was gay, I would tell them I was. They'd say, "Well, you're queer," and I would say, "So what?" That used to freak out a lot of people. People like me that are into being gay and dealing with Middle America have a lot of fun!

Have you dealt with middle america all your life?
It was very fashionable for black families in Youngstown, the hard, hard, hardcore working people, to have their babies baptized in the Catholic church. They sent their children to Catholic schools. Well, Mother decided to do that trip to me and I got alienated from black society, from the

blacks that lived in my neighborhood. I had to deal with all these white trips and white people and white people and white people and hear those divine nuns. Honey, the shit the nuns talked was much more intense than street talk. Nuns are some of the finest creatures on earth, very simple, very basic, very plain. They are into the same trips that I'm into: spreadin' love and joy, in nun drag. They personify the purity of women, which makes them very harmless. You didn't have to worry about dealing with them sexually or anything like that. They were just intense in their own trip, so intense they damn near had me convinced to join the nunnery, the male nunnery, the priesthood.

Church is very important. It's mankind's way of establishing spirituality. It's definitely as mind-controlling as any force on earth but the church does teach how to be nice to people and how to absorb the anger of other people.

How did you like working at the Garden Court?

Well, since I've been in San Francisco so many fantasies have been happening. I put in applications at all these hospitals and nobody hired me so I went to the waiters' union since I worked as a waiter while I was in school. Well, San Francisco is world-acclaimed for its restaurants, and with all these queens out here being waitresses, I thought, wow!, what's gonna happen? First they sent me out to Candlestick Park, to a little booth in the underbelly of the thing, and I dealt with a billion thousand people selling hotdogs and beer. It was Monday night at the football and the place was jammed, jammed, jammed, but it was on TV and everything so when they gave me a little break I went upstairs and smiled and posed in case someone saw me on TV.

The next day the union sent me to the Saint Francis Hotel for the annual San Francisco Opera Guild Luncheon, and every lady who walked through the door had $10,000 on her *someplace*, and they were all struttin' and profilin' and carryin' on. I mean divine, just divine. Well, I fitted into it like a T. I gave them just divine waiter trips. When I put a tray up, just rearin' back strutting, the only beard in the entire place and one of the few blacks, I got a lot of attention and I liked it. It really felt good. Well! I survived working a banquet in San Francisco, great! I felt such a major relief.

So that night I got assigned to the Sheraton-Palace Hotel and I walked into the Garden Court and freaked out! I said, "Oh my God, I'm not going to work here, there's no way all this could happen. What is this? I've got to really have it together."

The people who work here must be absolutely pissy at it, just divine. They have to do it to death." I just said, "Well, I'm simply going to have to do it too." Well, the grander I was, the more I strutted, the more sissified I was and everything else, the bigger and higher the tips! Of course, I was in formal attire, a nice ruffled shirt, and I looked good. I was just drinkin' my Jack Daniel's, which was the bar bourbon, of course, and servin' my guests, jokin' with 'em and so forth, and the maitre d' comes over and says, "Take good care of your guests, you have the general manager, the executive chef, and all staff people." Oh, no! After the way I'd been carryin' on with these people, 'cause I had the glow going, and then this guy gives me his card, and it says, "Executive Chef, Sheraton-Palace Hotel," and he said, "Come down in the morning and we'll give you a job." Well, I instantly freaked out. First thing I said to him was, "I don't want to shave my beard," and he said I didn't have to. Oh mercy, I hollered at people OOOww UUww aaaargh I loved it.

But you gave it up and went back into nursing...

I look so good in white! You should see it when I walk into these hospitals, they turn and look. Ohmygod, Doctor Kildare, eat your heart out. They should make a movie around me being a doctor. I enjoy putting on white uniforms and walking into a patient's room and saying, "Good morning, I'm Larry, I'm your nurse today." I can get a grip on that role because nursing is very, very, very basic. All you do is take care of somebody, be nice to somebody. When you're sick and laid up in a hospital bed, you really appreciate the slightest nicety. I get all that warmth and good feedback, so it reaffirms me as being a nice person. When somebody comes into the hospital crippled and leaves walking and you know you took care of them eight hours a day, you feel good about it.

7. The Raiderettes

Tuesday afternoon, six minutes to three. Scott sat at his desk in the bank, twirling his mustache and looking at the clock. In six minutes the bank would close, and he, as operations manager, would start checking the tellers out. He turned his attention to the new girl and watched her hesitate a moment before selecting a rubber stamp. She made her choice and applied it firmly to a check. *Please, please, please let her not make a mistake. Let me get out of here early today.*

BILL, SCOTT, AND DEMIAN

Fifteen miles north, across the Golden Gate Bridge, Bill sat at his desk, drumming his fingers on a page of foolscap copy, most of which had a large red X drawn across it. As a copywriter for a major legal publishing firm, his responsibilities include an endless stream of brochures, jacket covers, blurbs, introductions, whatever was needed. Bill wears his responsibility like his tie, naturally, without a second thought, but that afternoon his mind was elsewhere, perhaps drifting down

through the stands at the Oakland Coliseum where the Raiders play, down over the three decks of screaming maniacs to the edge of the playing field, to the band, to the cheerleaders, the Raiderettes.

Twenty miles east, across a different bridge, Demian sat at *his* desk in the big art studio where he teaches high schoolers the fundamentals of form and composition. The last class of the day had just cleared out and he was enjoying a moment's peace. He turned to gaze at a drawing on the wall, a charcoal Jesus, a gift from his most talented student, since gone on to art school in New York. It was Jesus smiling, knowing, moments before his betrayal.

Four o'clock. Scott cruised up Twin Peaks Boulevard on his motorcycle, heading for Bill's apartment. The new girl had had a perfect day with no mistakes. With a twist of his wrist he jetted up the mountain in the middle of the city, feeling higher and higher. *Tonight!*

Bill and Demian arrived at the same time from their jobs across the bay, and found Scott waiting for them, sitting astride his bike. For a moment the three men stood in the carport looking at the vast panorama of city and bay that spread out beneath them, each in turn stealing a glance at the others, trying to freeze the frame, remembering who they were.

Six hours later, wild and exuberant, they marched into the Halloween studio as the Raiderettes, high heels kicking, pompons flashing.

"Let's hear it for big number twelve! Rah *rah* RAH!"

WHOSE IDEA WAS IT TO DO THE RAIDERETTES?

Bill: One of the guys I have Raider season tickets with suggested the Raiderettes, but he didn't want to do it with us. At forty-nine he couldn't do a high kick very well.

ARE YOU ALL FRIENDS OR LOVERS OR WHAT?

Bill: We're friends.

Demian: We share a few excesses.

ARE YOU ALL GAY?

Bill: Well, as someone said, "If you're over twenty-five and living in San Francisco and single and male, it's assumed you're gay."

WHAT DREW YOU ALL TOGETHER AS RAIDERETTES?

All: Insanity! Craziness!

IS CRAZINESS YOUR WAY OF LIFE?

Bill: No, not really.

Scott: Speak for yourself! We've done a lot of partying together.

Bill: Scott's the outrageous one.

Demian: And I'm the other extreme. I'm

an old maid. I'm the most conservative.

Bill: In San Francisco you have to do something really outrageous to be considered outrageous. We're by no means outrageous.

Scott: I'm not prepared to say I'm not. I don't hide anything.

Demian: Well, you should.

WHO MADE THE COSTUMES?

Scott: I did the sewing. I had some extra black material and thought I'd give it a try. I ended up making all three skirts and the vests.

Bill: We bought the shirts in the Mission District because the most effeminate blouses we could find were in a men's store in the Mexican area. The boots we found at Lane Bryant, which is a tall women's shop. They were grey and we sprayed them white. Scott was the screw-up. He wears an eleven man's. The pompons were ordered from a professional pompon maker.

Do any of you ever go in drag?

All: No. Hell no. Never.

Would you wear your costumes to a raider game?

All: Nooo!

Bill: As a matter of fact, at one game there were these four very East Bay macho bullshit boring guys who must have seen us on Polk Street because they recognized me. There were all these little whisperings and then one of them threw a beer in my face. He ended up with a broken nose.

BILL

Bill was born and raised in San Antonio, Texas, and has lived in San Francisco seven years. His wry humor is delivered with a pleasant south Texas accent and an air of quiet confidence. Bill is a very conservative man who abhors the stereotype notion of gays as wild-eyed radicals. Halloween is the only time he goes out and carries on in the street.

WHEN DID YOU LEAVE TEXAS, BILL?
After graduate school, I left for the army. I
went through four years of ROTC.

WHAT BRANCH OF THE ARMY WERE YOU IN?
I was the public information officer and
copy editor of a brigade newspaper, north
of Saigon. A brigade newspaper would be
the equivalent of a small-town
newspaper. I was the only officer and
combat reporter on the paper, and I escorted
foreign and American journalists to the front,
if they wanted to go there. I got into a couple
of firefights, but I'm still here.

DID BEING GAY CAUSE YOU ANY PROBLEMS
WITH THE MILITARY?
In the army it probably caused less of a
problem than it does in civilian life, because
most of the military hierarchy is very naïve
about homosexuality. They probably assumed
that anyone who was gay wouldn't be in
there.

WHAT WERE YOUR POLITICAL SENTIMENTS
AT THE TIME?
I was probably kind of a right-wing
moderate. I've changed a bit but I'm still
fairly conservative. Oddly enough, many
gay people are. Of course, everybody in
the army was very anti-army, which was
very chic, unless they were career. After
Fort Hood, Texas, Vietnam was a pleasure.

DID YOU CHANGE WHILE YOU WERE THERE?
I was more against the war when I left,
but what changed drastically were my
feelings toward the Vietnamese people.
I did volunteer work at an orphanage when
I was there and I met quite a few
Vietnamese and they grew faces.

AND THE GAY LIFE?...

Oh, there was a fabulous gay bar in Saigon. Although I'm not attracted to small people sexually, I think, aesthetically, the Vietnamese are the most beautiful people on the face of the earth. Just to look at them, they're gorgeous. In Saigon both the men and the women were incredibly attractive.

To my knowledge, the Vietnamese society has no history of homosexuality per se. A person is not gay forever in Vietnam. It is just assumed that you will marry and father children and carry on the family line. All the gay people I knew had certain obligations and expected to fulfill them. They might have sexual dalliances on the side, which is not looked down upon as it is in the West.

HOW DID YOU COME TO LIVE IN SAN FRANCISCO?

I spent a month here after Vietnam, and it was a point of transition in my life. Before that, everything had been planned: college, graduate school, and the army, and then nothing, a complete void and a good time for a change. San Francisco is, I don't know, a state of mind, or nonmind, or what have you. It's a fabulous thing to experience when you are young. It's a great town to have fun in, but I keep my ties with Texas. I subscribe to magazines from Texas and keep in contact with people there. Essentially I am very south Texas, very conservative.

If I were straight I'd probably live in Marin County with two children and a two-bedroom house, and would come into the city for the theatre and the opera, and maybe the discos. I'll probably go back to Texas.

YOUR CONSERVATIVE LIFE-STYLE SEEMS TO BE IN DIRECT CONTRADICTION TO THE IDEA OF THE RAIDERETTES.

I don't think so. Halloween is like that. People let loose their wildest inhibitions. Once a year, the whole thing, the shopping, the sewing, the picking out makeup—I don't know makeup from borscht—but you run around and you pick up a few things and smear 'em on your face and you look fine. It's just entertainment.

DEMIAN

No one in the gay community suffers more from the stigma of homosexuality than the gay teacher. Many people who advocate gay rights balk at the notion of gays instructing the young.

Demian has taught for eight years in a suburban Catholic high school, all the while keeping an essential truth about himself carefully closeted. At the same time he has been producing a series of extraordinary drawings with a homosexual theme in preparation for a gallery showing.

WHAT DO YOU TEACH, DEMIAN?

I teach French, painting, and drawing.

WHAT WOULD HAPPEN AT SCHOOL IF YOU WERE DISCOVERED TO BE GAY?

I would lose my job. There are rumors flying around now, but that's to be expected. It's an all-boys school and they can be rather nasty little devils. I've had my classroom opened with keys and things have been written on my board. Some of our kids are vicious enough to try to push it through to the principal. You know, get proof, a witch-hunting kind of thing.

DO YOU WANT TO STAY THERE?

No, I'm looking for a way out, but being educated as a teacher and having spent the last eight and a half years teaching, my salability in the business world is minimal. One of the reasons I like teaching is that it's creative. It's the challenge of making a kid understand and accept something totally different. I like teaching, and any other field I get into would have to be creative, something that allows me to express the deep, creative compartments of my life.

ARE THERE ANY SCHOOL DISTRICTS ANYWHERE WHICH WILL HAPPILY ACCEPT GAY TEACHERS?

Not too many, if any. The city schools are liberal enough, but when I was doing graduate work at USF, there was a three-year waiting list.

YOU DESCRIBED YOURSELF AS THE MOST CONSERVATIVE OF THE RAIDERETTES...

I'm not generally outgoing. I'm very shy, very quiet, nothing abnormal, just a regular, boring human being who goes blithely on, except once a year. Bernice gives me a release once a year when I can be aggressive and obnoxious, which Bernice is.

The whole thing of Halloween for me is creating a character. It's a creative action which in this case is lived. Bernice has her own personality and her own set of morals and her own manner of dealing with people. She doesn't give a damn! She's already gone out and stopped buses and sat on the hood of a moving car and other outrageous things, all creative actions.

IS THE COWBOY ANOTHER CHARACTER IN YOUR REPERTOIRE?

Oh yes, that's Buck. Buck and Bernice are two extremes. Buck is still in the developmental stage. So far he's just a facet; he has no personality yet. Lately in my drawing I've been doing fantasy with the character of Buck in the back of my mind, so a lot of it has to do with the cowboy mystique. So far with the cowboy mystique the only depth I've gotten to is realism.

REALISM AS IN MARLBORO COMMERCIALS?

As in Marlboro commercials, as in very close-up of boots and spurs, or a very close-up of a torn pant cheek.

WHAT'S THE ATTRACTION OF THE COWBOY?

Oh, it's the same thing as Bernice. They're characters and people look at a character and assume it's real but it's not, it's created. It's the whole mystique of creating the Marlboro Man as "man."

WITH A RHINESTONE HEART?

Yeah. You can walk the street and see all these characters people are performing for the sake of others and it's fascinating. The attempt to draw them is a contribution to the mystique, but the next logical step is to

push the drawings to the point where they no longer show the stereotype image but rather show that it is a ludicrous image of reality.

WHAT IS THE SOURCE OF THE MYSTIQUE, THE STEREOTYPE COWBOY?
I guess·it was television in the mid-Fifties with the very virile cow-person and the concept of right and the concept of wrong. It goes back much further than the Fifties but the majority of people on the street got the majority of their concepts from television. What the media have done to us in terms of sexual stereotypes is scary.

DEMIAN WAS AN EARLY CHRISTIAN MARTYR. DO YOU IDENTIFY WITH HIM?
Oh, God, we're all martyrs waiting for the chance.

YOU TEACH IN A CATHOLIC SCHOOL. WHEN THIS BOOK IS PUBLISHED, YOU MAY HAVE YOUR CHANCE. ARE YOU CATHOLIC?
Yes.

DO YOU GO TO MASS?
Not very frequently, but I go.

IN THE EYES OF THE CHURCH YOUR SEXUAL LIFE IS A SIN. DO YOU SEE YOURSELF AS A SINNER?
No. I don't go to auricular confession. I don't think it's necessary for me. It's a very nice vehicle for people who have trouble being truthful with themselves, seeing the flaws in themselves. I guess I've reached a level in my life where I know very well what's wrong in my life. I know how I can be very nonpersonal or impersonal toward other people but, as I mature, those instances are becoming less and less frequent. Simply using another person, or abusing another person's feelings, I find totally wrong.

DO YOU COME FROM A CONSERVATIVE FAMILY?
Yes, I come from a very small town in Pennsylvania. I don't talk to my family about what I do. Until I was twenty-eight I was not comfortable with my identity as a gay man, but I came to San Francisco to do graduate work and for the first time I was able to go places and see things and just feel free. People didn't care if you were gay, straight, left-handed, or right-handed. It was much more relaxed.

When you first move into the whole gay situation in San Francisco, it all looks like glitter. It's so much fun and it's free and everything's out there and everybody loves you until you get into it for a while, and then you realize that unless you've got something stable in your life, whether it's your job or your own comfort with yourself or a lover or friends, it's deadly.

HOW DID YOU AVOID THE PITFALLS OF THE CITY?
Oh, we stumble on occasion. My life is not in a bar. My life does not collapse if I don't have a trick. I can be perfectly satisfied walking out of a bar by myself on Saturday night. I'm not compulsive about the whole sexual side. I don't go to the baths. I can stay around the house, I can draw, I can go for a walk, I can go downtown, I can do anything and not feel as if I'm missing something in a bar.

THAT'S A BEAUTIFUL STATEMENT OF SANITY.
Don't say that! That's the first sign you're going off the deep end when you think you're sane.

SCOTT

"The miracle mile" is a six-block stretch of Folsom Street through the industrial district south of Market Street. During the day it is trucks bumping over potholes, sweating warehousemen, and motorcycle cops swearing in the dust. At night, bleak and deserted, it is The Brig, The Ambush, The Arena, the leather bars. Cab drivers call it "chain lane," and it caters to affluent gay men with expensive motorcycles and leather costumes. On the miracle mile, what appears to be a motorcycle cop may very well be someone in California Highway Patrol (CHiPs) drag.

Scott started going to Folsom Street two years after arriving in San Francisco from Phoenix, Arizona. The leather bars appeal to his sense of masculinity. They present a definite challenge, a series of barriers both social and sexual which demand to be crossed. Scott is one who accepted the challenge. As he says below, he was once shy and introverted and had no friends, but having come to San Francisco and burst through innumerable barriers, he has discovered a sense of himself.

HOW OFTEN DO YOU WEAR YOUR LEATHERS? Not as frequently as I used to. In 1976 I had an affair with a man who was really into Folsom Street and the leather trip and I was not at all. I hadn't even been to Folsom Street and it freaked me out. I was a little scared, a lot scared, actually, but with his prodding I started going to the gym and I bought my motorcycle. It was during that time that I grew my mustache, which is now my pride and joy.

WHAT ABOUT THE PLASTIC RIVETS ON YOUR COAT? DO THEY HAVE ANY SPECIAL SIGNIFICANCE?

Plastic rivets? Plastic rivets? My rivets are not plastic!

WHAT? I THOUGHT BILL SAID THEY WERE PLASTIC.

'Cause he thinks they're tacky! They're heavy metal, as a matter of fact. They don't mean anything, they're just part of the costume. When I've got all my leathers on, including my high-rise boots, I've got $800 worth of clothes on. One thing about the Folsom Street bars—almost everyone I've ever met down there works—the joke is that you have to work to afford all the leathers.

WHAT DO YOU FIND SO ATTRACTIVE IN THE LEATHER MYSTIQUE?

Um, good question... masculine appearance, I feel like a man, just the appearance of... a man can look good, some men look fantastic in a hat, a leather cap or a Western hat or even a starched fatigue cap. It depends on the person. You see a lot of uniforms at leather parties. It's a big thing to get a CHiPs uniform and wear it, I mean all the way down to the motorcycle helmet. I've seen two gorgeous men that had the whole image perfect and it was really hot. The whole attitude is what does it. That's what makes a man attractive. The whole attitude of standing there and looking down your nose at somebody is an attitude that's so much fun. I get a charge out of getting into that attitude with someone, looking at

somebody and finding him attractive, and they've got this attitude and then going behind the attitude and seeing what they're really like. 'Cause the attitude is a barrier and I like to go across barriers, Lord knows!

WHAT'S THE MOST FORMIDABLE BARRIER YOU'VE EVER CONQUERED?
How do you want to go that? What route? Sexually?

ANY WAY YOU CHOOSE...
The biggest barrier I've ever crossed was the leather number. Seeing somebody in a leather bar that's coming across as very, very heavy or very, very macho, and being able to connect with him and go home and having a good time. Sexually, the biggest barrier I've crossed is fist-fucking. That was really outrageous, being both top and bottom. The top can—playing top is what I do most, is the way I come across in a bar, and it's a neat trip how someone can do that. Now, when I've played bottom I've been so far gone I don't even remember. I've been so wasted on either acid or Quaaludes that I don't remember, so I can't speak from the bottom end of it.

WERE YOU STONED ON HALLOWEEN?
No, not at all. Bill and Demian do not do drugs and I will not do drugs around them. I was not stoned at all and I had two people accuse me of being on speed. Just being the Raiderettes, we were all so wired. We did a Raiderettes show on Castro Street which stopped everybody. The police opened the street to traffic and we led cheers to close it, which they did. Because of the image I projected it was a total shock for people because I would go into the character of Gracie. You sit there and cross your legs appropriately and do the number with your hair to keep it out of your eyes. False eyelashes are a bitch: they're so goddamn heavy, they feel like they're hanging down to your feet.

I enjoy playing characters, and Gracie is just another character. Bill and Demian are two different people when they're in the Raiderette costumes, but I'm the same. I can be spotted no matter what. I don't change other than going into the female role, the walk, the gestures. I'm not afraid of being gay. In every job I've ever had since I left home, everybody's known that I was gay and I've had no bad vibes. The people that couldn't deal with it I ignored.

HAVE YOU BEEN LIKE THIS ALL YOUR LIFE? HAVE YOU ALWAYS KNOWN YOU WERE GAY?
No. I was extremely shy and introverted when I lived at home. I had no friends in school at all. I started thinking about homosexuality when I was about fourteen, fifteen, sixteen years old. When I first came out I was running around with a well-known gay man I had a crush on, and my brother found out and told me to stop or he'd beat the shit out of me. I ignored him.

DID HE BEAT YOU?
No, but he probably could have. Now he couldn't.

MANY GAY MEN WEAR HANDKERCHIEFS AND OTHER SEX-ROLE PARAPHERNALIA. DO YOU?
I did when I started going to the leather bars. It was just a sign, part of the costume.

WOULD YOU CARE TO RUN DOWN WHAT THE VARIOUS SIGNS MEAN?
Well, I'm only familiar with a few. Anything worn on the left, keys, handkerchief, what have you, is active, or top man; on the right, you're bottom, passive. A blue handkerchief is fuckor and fuckee, red is fist-fucking. Occasionally you'll see a white, which is a j.o. trip. Yellow is water sports, orange is anything, black is heavy S-and-M. You've got the light blue, the puce, a green, and a brown. The brown is scat. That's all I can remember.

8. The Night Porter

It's not unusual for a painter down on his luck to pick up a Master of Fine Arts degree, start working on a Ph.D., get married, have a couple of kids, quit school, and accept a teaching position. And it's not unusual for such a painter to hang on to his teaching job long enough to become the chairman of the art department in his college. Many people in this position are probably not painters at all, only technicians and professional students with no desire to leave the academic womb.

RICHARD

But Richard *is* a painter, so one day at the age of thirty-three he stuffed his wife and kids into the car, and left Wisconsin to start all over in San Francisco.

In a neighborhood of old warehouses south of Market Street, they discovered a community of artists living in lofts in an old, converted factory. One corner of his huge loft is strewn with all the customary painterly paraphernalia, while the rest is devoted to the amazing menagerie of wife and kids, several cats, a couple of birds, a dog,

and a rabbit. Often, several of the family's friends are over, many of whom are gay. Some, including Chuckie, Jeffrey, and Sully, are practicing drag queens.

WELL, RICHARD, ALL THE OTHER PEOPLE WE'VE INTERVIEWED ARE EITHER GAY OR BISEXUAL, AND HERE WE SEE A FAMILY. ARE YOU, BY ANY CHANCE, GAY OR BISEXUAL?
No, but almost all my friends are gay.

HOW DO YOU RELATE TO THE GAY PEOPLE THAT YOU KNOW?
Our interests are similar: painting, drawing, music, even, sometimes, shocking the public, things like that.

DURING THE SEVENTIES, GAY PEOPLE BECAME THE MOST FLAMBOYANT, OUTRAGEOUS MEMBERS OF THE AVANT-GARDE. IS THAT WHERE YOUR AFFINITY LIES?
Somewhat, at least the surface quality of things being outrageous and flamboyant. I think beneath that there's a great deal more. In the film on Quentin Crisp, *The Naked Civil Servant,* a lot of that flamboyance comes out of needing to identify your personality and needing to prove to society that you really exist. Recently several of us went out to dinner in drag to an expensive restaurant and then spent the evening around the city, and it's not only that outrageous flamboyance in public but you'll find there's a lot of fun in it! When other people in the restaurant are smiling they have something to talk about for the rest of the night. It's just looking for a way to enjoy society, enjoy the social structure rather than having to fit in like a cog where everybody else is and having to struggle with it. There's some fun to get out of it too.

WOULD YOU HAVE DONE THIS IN WISCONSIN?
I probably wouldn't have, no. I would have been something else. When the hippie movement was big in Wisconsin I dressed the role of that, but that became very tiring. Maybe at some point this will grow tiring, also. I think it's mostly been influenced by situation, living in San Francisco, having a lot of very close friends who are gay and who spend their time, at least their party time, in drag.

IN THE HIPPIE ERA, "STRAIGHT" MEANT SOMETHING OTHER THAN WHAT IT MEANS TODAY. TO MY WAY OF THINKING, YOU'RE PRETTY BENT, RICHARD.
Well, I guess I don't fit in in a lot of places. Even when we were living in Wisconsin I did not fit into your traditional straight society. I don't fit in completely in a gay society. I don't fit in completely in this community of artists, either, but this is the closest I've come to finding more than one or two people that I have things in common with. We share a lot of creative goals, and a lot of humor.

WHY DID YOU COME TO SAN FRANCISCO?
I have no idea. It was just a case of both of us quitting our jobs and going to a place we'd never been before. Leaving the Midwest, where I'd grown up, and quitting a job that I had trained myself to believe was important, was a total crisis. I was the chairman of a department and supposedly was fitting into all those little categories of success, and none of them were comfortable. I just gave all that up and moved here and ran out of money and everything just kind of fell apart. I was suicidal for a while, the whole thing, and went through therapy. Isn't it a state law that you have to have therapy when you move to California? I had become very suspicious and paranoid of everybody around me, but gradually I realized there were things I liked about myself, things I liked about San Francisco, things I liked about just about everybody.

A long time ago I heard that six months after a crisis the creative energies and ideas come pouring out, and six months after it happened I had more ideas than I knew what to do with. I used to feel that my work was only my own and gave back only to me and now I can see that perhaps it can give to other people.

WHAT DO YOUR KIDS THINK WHEN YOU GET DRESSED UP?
I've asked them about that, and it doesn't bother them at all. They see the humor in it. They're close friends with all the people I know. The only request I've had is from my youngest daughter, who asked that I not dye my hair blue or magenta. She doesn't think it would go over too well with her friends in her class, because I spend some time with her class taking field trips. They joke about it: Daddy's dress, Daddy's wig. They're probably the most broad-minded people I know.

HOW WOULD YOU DESCRIBE YOUR HALLOWEEN COSTUME?
Somewhat Italian, somewhat punk. A black leather jacket, a black top, black pants, black heels, black earrings, black, black, black, and very light whiteface.

WHY DID YOU SAY ITALIAN?
I guess that deals with the Italian makeup and the Italian hairstyles with a very severe look.

AND WHY PUNK? DO YOU WISH YOU WERE SEVENTEEN?
Yeah. I go to the Mabuhay Gardens and all the other punk clubs. I like looking for the punks.

HOW DID YOU LOOK WHEN YOU WERE SEVENTEEN? WAS YOUR HAIR SLICKED BACK?
Oh, yeah. It was parted on both sides with a jellyroll, the curl down the forehead in the middle, a ducktail in the back, black glasses, pointed shoes, and a white Pontiac convertible with chrome fender skirts, green leather interior, green convertible top, all that stuff.

WE'VE BEEN CALLING YOU THE NIGHT PORTER.
The Night Porter. Well, that's appropriate.
YOU LOOKED QUITE FEARSOME...
Well, thank you.

9. Lee and Juliette

Brian is hiding in the walk-in closet in the Jackie Kennedy Memorial Dining Room in B's apartment, rapidly opening and closing the door as if it were a bellows or a fan, pausing every few sweeps to peek out and flutter his eyelashes.

BRIAN AND B

"Can I come out of the closet now?"

A moment later he steps into the center of the room and assumes the role of aggressive young fashion designer.

"I want to promote my career," he states, and starts talking about his upcoming fashion show.

For Brian, the world of glamour and high fashion is not a remote fantasy; it is his life. He drops names like yarrow stalks; fondling them like tokens of good fortune. His manners are carefully manicured. His speech is carefully correct. His smile is carefully charming. Yet the bold outspokeness of this young man of twenty-four is not affected. His opinions are his own.

BRIAN

HOW WOULD YOU DESCRIBE YOUR

HALLOWEEN COSTUME, BRIAN?
B and I did two women, Lee and Juliette,
who live in the city. Lee cuts hair and
Juliette is a model. I design clothes and
the clothing I wore that evening was a
knock-off of a design that I sold to Lee,
whom I represented. I did my hair like
Lee, wore my makeup like Lee, and my
smock was reminiscent of a piece of haute
couture Lee wore socially very often. It
was the first time I ever dressed up in
such a fashion, but it was a conceptual
piece, more as sculpture than as a political
statement.

ORDINARILY YOU DON'T DRESS IN DRAG?
No, ordinarily I don't; however, I do
design costumes, not for men but for
people, and I believe everyone's clothing
is a costume, no matter how conservative
or liberal. You can play the part of a
businessman, a career woman, a house-
wife, a bum, and I think they are all
equally creative. Some of them are looked
at socially as higher or more refined art
forms. Some people are able to appreciate
a designer's work. Haute couture is the
life-style of people who desire excellent
clothing, and that's how I make my living.

WHAT DO YOU USUALLY DO ON HALLOWEEN?

Usually I do something much more fantasy. I've been a pumpkin. I've been an eggplant. Certainly I acknowledge that men wear drag, not so much that I think it's a life-style that's *real*, but I do try to appreciate other people's fantasies and try to see them as part of what they're working on in their own lives.

WHAT DID YOU THINK OF THE ENTIRE EXPERIENCE OF HALLOWEEN ON POLK STREET?

I think Halloween on Polk Street has become everything except the joyous fantasy that I believe Halloween is meant to be. It's become violent. It's become a voyeur's sport. I think a decadence has set in in San Francisco where people who are very much in disagreement with people getting dressed up come out to violently oppose what they see. It's very unfortunate that a good contingency of people come out to inflict harm.

HOW DID YOU BECOME A FASHION DESIGNER?

Well, I could never figure out what to wear and I was always interested in what people were wearing. One day on the bus a friend and I were looking in store windows as we were driving past and I asked my friend, "Do I have to go to school if I want to design clothes, or can I just draw pictures and have them made?" And pretty perplexed by the question he said, "Hmm, I think you have to go to school," and so I went home and ran my finger down the fashion schools in the phonebook and called one up, had my interview, got my money to them and went to school. I've been doing two shows a year for six years and I have a show coming up in August.

ARE YOU GAY, FOR THE RECORD?

For the record, my experiences have been many. All my life I have been opposed to labels. If you were going to label me as gay, my latest desire is not for a man. Let me say, if you can decipher this, that Mondays, Wednesdays, and Thursdays are gay, Tuesdays, Fridays, and Saturdays are heterosexual, and Sunday is something better than both. I would rather avoid a label of gay. I would rather avoid a label of bisexual.

I always thought, while growing up, that women would be attracted to men that were dull and supposedly deep and strong and dark and large and quiet, and I was always skinnier than macho. Now I find that women are very much interested in men, in my own experience, who are a little more flamboyant, a little more honest, showing a little bit more of their feminine side and the ability to impress them with their masculine beauty instead of their masculine duty.

Before I, if I may, came out of the closet, I was always trying to be a product, a creation of somebody else's will. When I finally realized a few years ago that I am who I am, I decided to be it freely. I would rather say that Brian is perfectly himself.

B

At the far edge of society, there are no rules, only possibilities. This is the province of psychic sabotage and surrealism. This is the land of B.

In a sense, B does not exist at all, for B is a wholly fictional character, a manufactured personality *lived out* by his creator. B is an instance where an artist and his work have completely merged.

B's art is a continual performance in which the tiny rituals that make up our lives are dramatized to reveal their absurdity. He sees absurdity everywhere. It would be easy to turn such absurdity to despair, but instead he turns it to satire and comedy.

Drag forms a great part of the character of B, but it is only the costuming in the general atmosphere of theater that surrounds him. With B one expects the unexpected: one never knows just what he is capable of, but surely it will be something spontaneous and poignant. Once he stayed up all night in a drunken orgy with two friends and tape-recorded the entire event.

B first gained notoriety by walking around the campus of Indiana University, in Bloomington, Indiana, with a dress over his shirt and pants. He describes Bloomington as a rather repressed place, which was what inspired him to perform such a bizarre act.

In 1978 he won The First Annual Outrageous Beauty Contest in San Francisco when he appeared in Jackie Kennedy drag.

When we interviewed B in the Jackie Kennedy Memorial Dining Room in his apartment on ritzy Nob Hill, we had the feeling he was putting us on. He refused to take himself seriously. He would mumble unintelligibly for several moments and then say something with astonishing clarity, as if for our benefit he were reinventing B on the spot.

HOW OLD ARE YOU, B?
Do I have to tell the truth?

YOU CAN LIE IF YOU WISH.
Let's say I'm twenty-five. Maybe in ten years I'll up it to thirty.

ARE YOU WORKING THESE DAYS?
I had a job in a law library but I got laid off, so I'm on vacation. I've had other jobs, boring clerical jobs and worker's jobs. I haven't had any ambition since I took LSD. I suppose I'll have to go back to work but I'm not really fond of it.

WHAT ARE YOU FOND OF?
"I Love Lucy," and getting lots of sleep.

IS SLEEP YOUR MAIN FORM OF RECREATION?
Yeah, I love to sleep. And I'm writing an autobiography of B.

IT SEEMS B BECAME VERY FAMOUS AS…
We're still working on *very* famous.

…AS A DRAG QUEEN, OR WHAT WOULD YOU SAY?
Well, drag was a part of the personality, the manufactured personality of B, the image. Drag is very much a part of the image but it's not exactly the image of a drag queen.

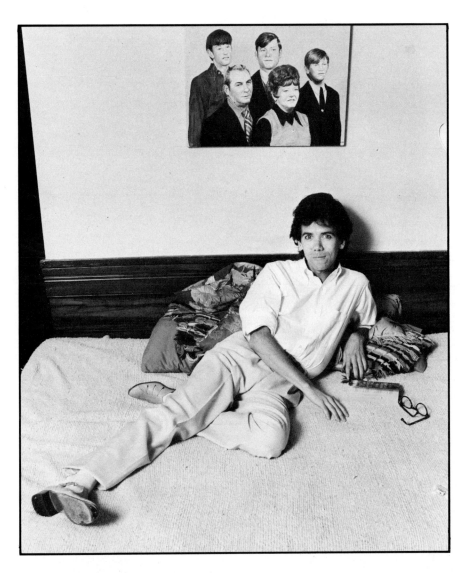

WHAT ARE THE COMPONENTS OF THE IMAGE?
Art and absurdity. The absurdness of the drag is what perpetuates it. I've made lots of appearances but I've never taken it seriously. I'm always detached and kind of plastic. It's always entertainment. There's no psychodrama going on. I'm not living out any fantasies. It can be very spectacular and glamorous, you know, I can take it or leave it. Even though it's perpetuated itself over the last few years, I've never been that attached to it. It just kept happening and I was more or less forced into it by friends who enjoyed it and wanted more.

DID YOU BEGIN TO MANUFACTURE B IN SAN FRANCISCO?
No, it started in Bloomington when I was in college, and then I wasn't manufac-

turing it, I was living it. It was very gender-fuck to appear on the streets in drag, not real drag, just the accoutrements, wearing a dress over a pair of pants and going to class, that kind of thing. I was the center of attention when all this was going on but I always knew I could flip over the roles if I wanted to. It was nothing deep or meaningful, but it shocked a lot of people.

WHEN YOU GO IN DRAG, DO YOU FEEL AS THOUGH YOU ARE IMPERSONATING A WOMAN? ARE YOU GOING TO FOOL ANYBODY?
Oh, I'm sure I used to fool lots of people, but some I didn't. It doesn't bother me. I didn't want to *be* a woman, just dress up.

With me, physiologically since I'm so small, small bones and small face, it would be very convincing for me to look like a woman if I really tried, but I always make a point of acting a little more gruff in drag than I usually do, you know, sitting around with my legs apart, smoking cigars, guzzling beer. That always gets a laugh.

DO YOU GO IN DRAG MUCH ANYMORE?
Not as much as I used to. I go in drag when people least expect it, and people know that when I do drag, it's unusual and varied. I used to do it a lot when it was a novelty, but not anymore. Since I made a name for myself, I only do it on rare occasions, and Halloween.

WHAT'S THE MOST OUTRAGEOUS THING YOU EVER DID?
Well, a friend of mine started a literary magazine called *White Arms,* which was a very Dadaist kind of thing built around the persona of B. I was in every issue and in fact there was one whole B issue. We did a B coloring book, too, but the most outrageous thing was in the magazine. In 1971 or 1972 there was a Gay Liberation dance in Bloomington and I went as Jackie Kennedy at the assassination in a pink, blood-spattered suit and wig and pillbox. I've always been fascinated with her.

WHY?
Mainly the image, it's a highly manufactured image and she does it pretty well and keeps it under control. She wants her privacy and the attention. In the magazine we reenacted the assassination and photographed her crawling over the back of the car in her pink suit.

ARE YOU HAPPY YOU'RE IN SAN FRANCISCO?
Not really. Ever since I've been here I've felt like I was in transit, like in limbo, you know, purgatory, kind of stuck here until the next thing happens. I've been here five years and I still don't know what I'm doing. I keep thinking I'm going somewhere else, but I'm stuck here. I was going to Los Angeles last fall, but at the last minute I backed down. I need someone else to make the decision for me.

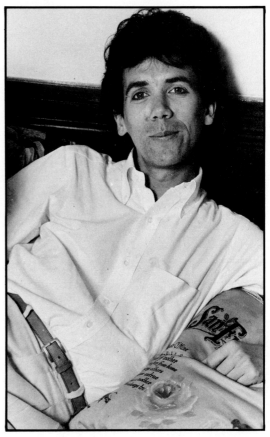

10. Ronnie

East Oakland is an ordinary working-class neighborhood fifteen miles across the Bay Bridge and down the freeway from San Francisco. The detached houses have driveways and garages,

ROSS

backyards and front porches, kids on skateboards and old folks out for a stroll. It could easily be part of Brooklyn or Cincinnati. Spiritually, it is light-years away from the bars and discos of Polk Street.

Ross lives here in a house he shares with a woman, Jeanette, ten years his senior, a few blocks from where he was born eighteen years ago. Jeanette is his biggest fan. "When Ross is in drag," she says, "look out, Farrah!"

When they first met, Ross was going to high school as Ronnie. With his fashion model's face and thin, gangly body, he has never had any problem passing as a woman. He walked into a beauty parlor where Jeanette was having her hair done. "Wow," she said to the beautician, "who is that beautiful chick?"

The neighbors are used to seeing Ross in makeup and Jeanette in her overalls, crawling under one of her half-dozen old Fords—just a happy suburban couple, both working, she as a night loader in a soda-pop factory, he as a fry-cook in a fast-food joint, living pleasantly with their pet boa constrictor, their hot rods, and their little eccentricities.

Are you ronnie or ross around the house!
Okay, there's Ronnie, there's Ross, and there's me, and I'm me. I do crazy things, you know, we all do, but I enjoy making people laugh. I don't want them to laugh particularly at me, but I want 'em to laugh with me.

WHEN YOU GO OUT, DO YOU EVER WEAR THE LEASH?
No, never. That's just something that happens once a year, on Halloween. I get dressed a lot, but it's just something I like to do. I have a lot of faces. I like to walk around and quote *Vogue.* I want to be a model. Sometimes I like to look like some of these other women I've seen: big, false eyelashes and heavy makeup and really look fancy. You don't do that every day but when you get the chance you really vamp it up. It's just people expressing themselves and how they feel at the time.

How often do you put on makeup?
It depends on how I feel. If I start to get a little high or I'm just sitting around the house and have a lot of energy and feel like being crazy, I'll go and put on some makeup. It's just a spontaneous reaction.

How old were you when you discovered you weren't quite like everybody else?
I'd say I was around eleven when I realized what was goin' on inside my head. I figured I was a real weird one, the one who felt two feelings, like a split personality in a way. Sometimes I get real crazy and I feel like doin' something and instead of thinking about I shouldn't do it, 'cause my mother brought me up to do what I want to do, I'd run off and do it. Eventually, I grew into it. I went to Stanford and went through tons of money, tons of therapy, everything, trying to get a sex change. After going through this long program for months and months, I got a letter that said they weren't going to do anything to physically change me at all until I graduated from high school with a B average. That really blew me away. I felt real cheated, and I thought, "I don't have to put up with that bullshit," and I didn't. I went to the head supervisor of the school board, I went in there flamin' and I said, "I can't go to school," and he said, "Oh, I can understand why. Don't." I went out that night and got smashed and went over to a friend's house and had all my hair cut off.

Do you think they refused to do a sex change because you were so young?
Yeah, that might have had something to do with it. I wasn't really sure. I felt, like, why should I have to wait? Other people waited and it was their own fault for not realizing earlier what they were. That space in my mind I'm trying to stay away from and leave very open 'cause it's a lot of feelings I'm real scared of there. I want to do modeling.

I want to be a model worse than anything in the world and I figure I can model female makeup and stuff and try to make the ads. Or I can male model. I'd really like to do both 'cause I'm positive I can make money at it. So when I walked into your studio I thought, "Wow! Here it comes, I'm finally getting my big break," so I really got into it. I really dug it with all the cameras around and the lights and the music and being high on top of it. I just thought, "Wow! Here it comes."

How long did you go to school as Ronnie?
Almost a year, until I quit. I never did really have any problems. It was a new school and I just enrolled as Ronnie. I always felt that a couple of girls that I knew had an idea. I had a couple of guys tell me I had a real deep voice. I wasn't as tall as I am now. I'm six two and in the last two years I've grown three and a half inches. I always kept myself where I wouldn't be put in any kind of situation where they would have any kind of idea at all.

How did you avoid P. E.?
Listen, if I don't want to do something, I don't do it. There is no way they can drag me out of my house and drag me down to that field and make me play P.E. if I don't want to. My mom is not gonna get out there and make me work my ass off. It seems ridiculous to me to get out there and lift weights and push bars and stuff just to show you can do it. I had a completely different life outside of school. I was always in San Francisco and partying and stuff. I'm an extremely hyper person.

How do you get along with all your straight neighbors?
Just fine. They're so naïve, they just don't realize what's going on. You have to be a really loud person, I mean stomp down the street in pink tights and wear hats before they'll get the idea. A lot of them could sit and talk to you for half an hour and then say, "Let's go to a bar and get some girls." I figure when I walk around, no matter where I am, the world's opened up enough so that if I see a married couple and I want to smile at him I'm goin' to, and if he sees me he sees me and that's how it works. I go out a lot, not as a woman anymore, not to bars, but to parties where everybody knows me and knows what's goin' on. It's pretty easily accepted because I'm such a loud, wild person. I do just exactly what I please.

11. The Boys with Bad Taste

In his work as a chauffeur for a wealthy San Francisco family, Jeffrey is surrounded by conventional, expensive good taste. The Mercedes, the Jaguar, the Louis XV chaise lounge, the Christian Dior finery—it's all very boring.

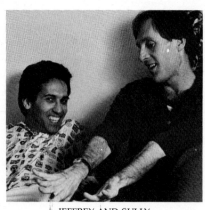

JEFFREY AND SULLY

But 1957 *Real Romance* magazines, old Fiestawear and Harlequin china, and (gasp!) Aunt Jemima cookie jars—Wow! That's the stuff of life! Rich people don't know anything about that. They're too busy being Republicans and getting their names in the society pages to go digging around in old *Vogues* for new drags. Ahhh, they don't know what they're missing.

Jeffrey and Sully live together in a spacious storefront apartment loaded to the rafters with kitsch. They collect junk, then sell the collections if they can and give them away if they can't. Once it was plastic high-heeled pumps, another time plastic handbags, then the china, the magazines, and the Aunt Jemimas.

One day Jeffrey was sitting around

the campus of Ohio State University, bored with school, when a friend said, "Let's go to San Francisco." "Okay," said Jeffrey, "where's that?"

Three days later Jeffrey was walking down Market Street still not quite sure where he was. He walked into a second-hand store to check out the local junk. Sully ran the store. Boy met boy, *Real Romance* jumped off the magazine rack, and they've been together ever since.

JEFFREY

DID YOU MAKE YOUR COSTUME?
No, I found it at Goodwill. I buy everything at Goodwill, or the Salvation Army

or something like that, thrift stores. I'm a fanatic thrift-store shopper. I used to go three times a day, but since I've been working I can only go once a day. I used to work at City Hall and there was Saint Anthony's on Golden Gate, and the Salvation Army at Seventh and Mission, and at lunchtime I could go to Sixth and Howard, 'cause after lunch there was nothing usually there. But Twenty-sixth and Valencia's open Monday, Wednesday, and Friday at night so I can go after work.

I believe in exploiting bad taste.

EXPLOITING BAD TASTE?
Yeah, I like that a whole lot. I believe in bad taste. I appreciate it in different senses.

WHAT IS BAD TASTE?
It's just, oh, nonprofessional-looking is bad taste to me, I guess. I think the Italians are the best at having bad taste.

WHY ITALIANS?

I guess because I grew up in Youngstown, Ohio, which is heavy Italian, heavy Mafia, and you see a lot of bad taste. My mother's third husband is Italian and I know his parents and they live in a trailer and have bad taste and I like that. I like that a lot so I buy things that are bad taste because they are bad taste. I buy Aunt Jemima stuff and *Real Romance* magazines and old *Vogue*s. I guess one of the things I mean by bad taste is that *Vogue* dictates a style and to alter that style is to make it "bad," 'cause *Vogue* is taste and not-*Vogue* is bad taste. The less *Vogue* you get the badder you get which means the more I like it, in a sense.

A LOT OF PEOPLE DRAW THE LINE AT "VOGUE"...

Oh, yeah. It's a life-style, *Vogue* is, like disco. It's great.

BUT YOU'RE ANTI-"VOGUE"...

In my appreciations, I'm anti-*Vogue*. I like anti-*Vogue* but I would prefer to be *Vogue*. It's a life-style, just like there's DR life-style. There are entire people whose lives are Design Research.

I always used to do bad drag and I would buy things that were bad although now it's almost in to be bad. You know, it's very punk, which I don't like. The punks don't research their bad taste. You have to know what good taste is to know what bad taste is. The only punks I know are real dumb. I don't appreciate what they are saying because they don't know where they are coming from, but that's only in a visual style. I don't know anything about their politics because I don't get involved in politics.

How about gay politics?
No. They always get schmaltzy. They get too cliché too fast and I just can't do it.

What do you get involved in?
Drag. That was really my art form for a long time.

Do you drag often or just on Halloween?
Oh, not just Halloween. For occasions like Christmas or Thanksgiving or somebody's birthday. I used to have a collection of plastic purses and a big collection of high heels that were all like Lucite and plastic. Finding a pair of shoes that fits is tough if you're big. There are drag stores, but most people who go for that don't have that kind of money. Most drag queens are all messed up and on SSI or something. They don't think they fit in. There's a bar downtown that's not a drag bar but a bar for male prostitutes who dress up like women, and these people are real. I like to go there. I like those people but they don't like me. They probably think I'm there to look at them. Not really, I sympathize with them entirely. I don't go in drag but just to look at bad drag, but they're pretty good. They always show a lot of leg. Legs are pretty easy to make look good. You can cover up your stomach but your legs usually hang out.

SULLY

Do you share Jeffrey's enthusiasm for bad taste?
Oh, yeah, I enjoy bad taste as much as Jeffrey. I enjoy going to junk stores and thrift shops and collecting paraphernalia and things.

Is that where you got your Halloween costume?
Everything except the wig. I guess I bought the stockings new. Everything else is second-hand. Drag queens have always been big on thrift shops. You find big shoes and things like that much cheaper. Either that or you make it. It's too expensive to buy new things.

There aren't too many wealthy drag queens, are there?
No. It's hard to make a living that way. I went to a drag show the other night, and part of the thing was if you liked the performer you gave her a dollar bill, and there was this woman sitting in front of me who was passing out dollar bills to everyone. Maybe thirty dollars, and I thought, "My God, this must be this queen's whole SSI check." I couldn't believe it.

How long have you been going in drag?
I've only been doing it since my birthday last year. That was my first time in drag. Not my first time in costume but my first time in drag.

You've lived with Jeffrey…
For about eight months but we've known each other for a long time.

You strike me as a man easily bored…
Well, yeah, people say that about me.

What piques your interest, holds your attention?
For how long? A movie will hold my attention for two hours.

Do you read books?
I'm not much of a reader. I'm more visual than literary. I used to be a painter. I guess doing a drawing will keep my attention, something like that. And bad taste holds my interest.

Are you political at all?
No. I guess vaguely political, but not really. I think people are more interested in living life than in political ideals or something. Political ideals are hard to live with. I was semi-political when I was in college, but that was very useless. I guess I've never really understood the whole thing very much.

12. The Girls from Hunter's Point

Hunter's Point is a tiny spit of land that sticks out into the bay five miles south of downtown. Once a sprawling naval base covered the point, but the navy abandoned the base, and the housing projects, built for shipyard workers during World War II, were taken over by the city. The dilapidated buildings, with sagging roofs and plywood windows, form the heart of what is, by most people's reckoning, the worst and most dangerous neighborhood in San Francisco. The streets go unrepaired.

LUTHER AND LEON

Rats and cockroaches battle human beings for living space. In no way does it resemble the San Francisco of cable cars and pretty bridges.

Yet thousands of people stay in Hunter's Point for generations by choice, because it's home, because it has the best weather in San Francisco, because, like any inner-city village, it has its own code, its own personality, its own web of friends and family and deep-rooted connections. The people of Hunter's Point are well aware of its reputation

as a place to avoid. They make no excuses for the violence, except to point out that their business is their business and outsiders should simply stay away.

We had no illusions when we went to see Leon and Luther in their home on Hunter's Point. When we found the address on obscure Harbor Road, it appeared to be the only occupied apartment in an otherwise abandoned project building. We thought we were walking into a trap. Bye-bye, Nikons. Bye-bye, Sony. And then Leon appeared out of nowhere, smiling, holding up a half-quart of beer and waving for us to come in.

We entered a tiny apartment absolutely jammed with people. Luther's mother, the glorious, resplendent Anna Mae, gave us a rousing welcome, introduced the cousins and brothers and daughters and friends, gave us beer, smoked our dope, and made us feel right at home.

LUTHER

WERE YOU BORN AND RAISED HERE ON HUNTER'S POINT?
That's right.

IT SEEMS AS THOUGH YOU HAVE A VERY WARM AND LOVING RELATIONSHIP WITH YOUR MOTHER...
I think my mother is the best mother anybody could ever have, 'cause we understand each other.

HAVE YOU ALWAYS HAD THIS UNDERSTANDING?
Always, 'cause, see, when I got about twelve—I matured fast—I asked my mother could I smoke, and she said yeah, 'cause she knowed I was gonna do it behind her back anyway. So a couple of years after that, I just sat down with my mother talking, 'cause I would buy all these sandals and hide 'em, so I just told my mother I was gay, and she said that was all right, she still loved me. Whatever I wanted to be I should try to be the best at it. I didn't start publicizin,' people didn't start knowin' 'til I was about fifteen. Once I let people know what was happenin' they let me alone.

HOW OLD ARE YOU NOW?
I'm twenty-one. I'm really twenty and a half.

DID YOU GRADUATE FROM HIGH SCHOOL?
Uh-huh, but I was always raised to be me, see, and I'd go to school and be me, and I couldn't be bothered with all the commotion that the kids were givin' me, so I'd leave school and go to another school. My mother always taught me, if you want to wear this or that, wear it, just be you, 'cause I'm her son, and anything that I do is all right with her. So I was more like, what you would say, independent. I was just doin' me. I'd like to explore, so I dropped out of school and me and Leon were doin' a little modeling, then I went back and got my diploma.

Do you and leon live together?
Yeah.

Are you lovers?
No, we're like brothers.

Tell us a little about your halloween costume.
Okay. We got together and decided this time we were going to be bizarre, so we all got chiffon and leotards only different colors and everybody made their own top, and then we made up our faces real pretty, but—wow!—I couldn't really tell you what kind of image I was tryin' to give you, but I was calling myself a white woman, 'cause I was all in white. I was bein' more like a ghost, an up-to-date ghost, a mod ghost, the white woman, see. I enjoyed it. We got high and all that week we costumed and went to Halloween parties.

WE'VE TALKED TO MANY YOUNG PEOPLE
YOUR AGE WHO LIVE DOWN IN THE
TENDERLOIN WITH NO FAMILY OR ANYTHING.
YOU'RE A VERY LUCKY YOUNG MAN...
Yeah, I know. A lot of those childs are
fifteen, sixteen years of age. That's what
I mean about my mother being understanding. A lot of them, their mother put
them out. It took Leon's mother a long time
to understand. That's why he moved in
with me. His mother told him he couldn't
be like that, and we just made her
understand that that's the way he's going to
be and he's not going to change at all. Now
she accepts it and it ain't nuttin.'

DO YOU GO OUT AND PARTY A LOT?
I like to go dancin.' I like to dress and go out
dancin.' I like designer clothes, both men's
and women's clothes. All my clothes
coordinate. I buy 'em like that. When I buy
a suit I make sure somethin' on that suit will
go with somethin' I got. That's what
dressing is all about, creating, and I create.
We like to dress like the magazines, *GQ* and
like that. We don't drag much anymore. We
used to when we was young, but we didn't
go all the way and wear fake breasts and all
that, but we wore skirts and boots. We were
more mod, just wow!, but I don't like to
shave off my mustache. I takes my mother
out to gay bars and she dances. She's very
uppity, she's cool. Me, I like all generations.
I can hang with any group and have a good
time. I like white, black, Chinese, all
people. People is people. We just all people.

LEON

HOW LONG HAVE YOU LIVED HERE WITH
LUTHER AND HIS FAMILY?
Three years.

WHY DID YOU MOVE IN?
Well, okay, from jump street, the
beginning, me and my mother were having
catty little problems, like, uh, like, I don't
like the hours you keep. Things of that
nature. I had been acting peculiar, staying
out all night, and different guys would stay
over. Some would be black and some
white and some Jewish, 'cause I go for

all races. When the problem arose
that I was going to let them know I was gay,
I told her point blank. This was when I was
sixteen and came to my senses. I let the
whole family know at one time, at the
dinner table. There was a lot of crying and a
lot of cold, hard treatment, but I was
becomin' a man so I got out on my own.
Since Luther was my closest buddy and
lifelong friend, I decided to move in with
him.

WHAT'S YOUR RELATIONSHIP WITH YOUR FAMILY NOW?
Oh, we're ace cool and blooming. Me and my mother are born in the same horoscope, Taurus. She wants me to move back in.

DO YOU GO IN DRAG VERY OFTEN?
I like dressing, but sometimes I feel different ways. Sometimes I want to look like a boy so I'll look like a boy. Sometimes I want to feel and look like a girl, then I look like a girl. And sometimes I get in the middle and feel like I want to look halfway, like, so to speak, I might have on some Levis and brogans, but at the top I might have on a tam or beret slightly tilted back across my head. I have three holes in my ear, and I might have an earring in each

hole, so that would make me look more like what we call "fish."

WHAT IS "FISH?"
That means a lady, a woman, a girl, a female.

HOW DID YOU FEEL ON HALLOWEEN?
Oh, I felt like a woman, I guess. I felt kinda half and half 'cause a lot of times I've went into drag but I've never worn titties or anything. I always wanted you to know what I was doing and respect the beauty of it. Now I'm an adult, I'm twenty-two, and I have a whole adult attitude on how I want to look and how I want to be presented to someone. I wouldn't want to call myself a fish name and not look like a lady.

Tell us about being gay and living in Hunter's Point…

Well, Hunter's Point is really a little black book full of mysteries and people that want to be and people that dip and dab. We have a lot of guys that dip and dab that don't want nobody to know, which is cool 'cause they respect us for bein' real, and we're always real. Realness is the ultimate, it's a twenty-four-hour thing.

We live out here and grew up out here and people that are around us, they can be enemies such as boys growin' up who don't know about the gay life, you know, and really don't know that people are going to be people regardless of how you feel about 'em or what you say about 'em. With all that goin' on we, like, sort of so to speak, fought our way through that.

You must have literally fought your way through.

Definitely. Luther and I both come from large families, with a lot of brothers and sisters and cousins, and outsiders come in and say somethin' or do somethin' and they don't know that this person is a brother or a cousin or a great friend, and then there's a hassle. Like on Halloween, a lot of our friends from the neighborhood turn out for something big like Halloween, and we're respected because we come from such a hard neighborhood. A lot of teenagers, and some adults, too, crowded around us and pretty much acted like a shield against other neighborhoods. People would see us coming, and they'd go, "Oh, no. Don't mess with them. They're the girls from Hunter's Point!"

Are there many gay people in Hunter's Point?

Sure. Everybody's gay. As far as being gay, to me, every man, and I'm a man, can be had at the proper time and the proper place, whether it be liquor to influence him or just another pretty guy. I've learned that a man knows exactly what another man wants. He has to know, he's a man, and if he doesn't, he's not a man. On the other hand, I haven't messed around with a girl since I was twelve, but if a situation came around and I was trapped in with a girl, something would happen, automatically. She'd have to do something and I'd have to do something.

Are there any gay women in Hunter's Point?

I can only put my finger righteously on one. We have generations on Hunter's Point. We like the sunshine and the view.

As a native san franciscan, what do you think of all the gay people coming into town?

They take all the jobs.

13. George

George appeared on Halloween as a ravishing spectre in blue, a vision of sartorial elegance utterly unexpected in a young man of nineteen. Like his friends Luther and Leon, George pays careful attention to matters of dress and appearance. As a student of cosmetology, he is applying the finishing touches to his innate and relaxed sense of style. Tremendously poised and dignified, he is, in the vernacular of California newspeak, "very together."

He lives with his aunt and cousin in

the pleasantly middle-class Excelsior district of San Francisco amidst comfortable and supportive surroundings. While his aunt and cousin, a lovely young woman, bustled about their fashionably appointed house, George sat in the kitchen and calmly spoke about his brief but unusual life.

HOW DID YOU MEET LEON AND LUTHER?

I met them downtown, in front of a club. I happened to be walking in front of a club where they happened

to be standing outside and we
gathered a friendship together.

THEY ARE REALLY INTO STYLE. ARE YOU?
I like to look nice, even if it means being
out of style. I feel, if you can't accept me
as George out of style, how can you accept
me as George in style? Leon and Luther
have been a big help. They always make
me feel comfortable.

DID YOU MAKE YOUR HALLOWEEN COSTUME?
No, my good friend and cousin made it
for me. The costume was first conceived
by me and the gang. We all wanted to
look like different colored balloons, but a
bit bizarre and risqué, so we got silk chiffon
and leotards and Charles Jourdan shoes,
the whole works. It cost about a hundred
and fifty dollars.

THAT'S EASILY THE MOST EXPENSIVE
COSTUME IN OUR GROUP...
Well, we like to have the best look in town,
so sometimes we work a little bit harder to
get something we want a little bit more.

DO YOU DRAG OFTEN, OR JUST ON
HALLOWEEN?
I used to do it whenever I felt it, but I was
young and didn't have to worry about
what people thought of me. I find that as
I grow older I'm joining a more conservative
bracket. If they want a drag queen, I give
them a drag queen. Once in a while I may
wear makeup to a party, but never full drag.

When I was fourteen, I used to sneak out
of the house and have a good time downtown, impersonating a woman, or trying to,
because I guess I came across like a
teenage girl. Guys have always mistaken
me for a girl no matter how masculine I try
to look. It was always easy for me to attract
women, and it was hard to get a man's
attention, so what's a better way than to
be a woman?

FOURTEEN IS PRETTY YOUNG. WERE YOU EVER HASSLED BY THE POLICE?
Never. I always minded my own business. It wasn't like I was out there being a hooker or anything. I was having a good time. I never really had any leashes put on me. I could always come and go as I pleased and do what I wanted to do. When younger people seemed turned off with me, I naturally went with older people who helped me get my head together. I was kind of wild and crazy for a while, but after a while I didn't want to be involved in the craziness anymore. I wanted to know what life is all about and I'm still lookin'!

I would like to go to Europe to see what their life-style is all about. Everybody tells me I'm so European, so I'll go over there and see if I am.

IS THAT YOUR PLAN FOR THE IMMEDIATE FUTURE?
Well, in two weeks I'll be through with cosmetology school, and then I'll take my state exam and become hairdresser to the world.

IS HAIR YOUR SPECIALTY?
It's not really my specialty, but it's a way of releasing my artistic ability. I prefer makeup. Some people release their feelings in a book or on an easel, I like to release mine on a person.

DID YOU MAKE UP LUTHER AND LEON ON HALLOWEEN?
No, I didn't. Everybody's design was their own. The concept was together but we all did our own individual artistic design.

HOW DO YOU GET ALONG WITH YOUR FAMILY?
Well, compared to most other classified "gays"—I don't like to be classified as "gay" or as anything—I'm still well loved and accepted in my family. My parents will help me as long as I'm going to school and doing something constructive for myself.

I've never turned against them which seems to be the fashion right now. Once I was aware of myself and they were aware of me, they were even more supportive.

WHEN DID YOU BECOME AWARE OF YOURSELF?

I was always aware of myself, even when I dated women, which I still do occasionally, but there was always something inside of me that said, "Why are you so attracted to men? Handsome men at that." I learned to be more self-confident just being alive in the world. For a while I was kind of scatter-brained. I always felt pressurized, even by society, to try to be such a perfect child, that it felt good to be wild. And I did get out there! I hung out. I was friends with everybody and they called me sissy and fag but they still liked me. I get called gay, and I guess it sounds better than homo-sexual or faggot. You know, my name is George; it's always been George and I've always refused to let anyone call me anything other than George, for the dignity of myself and my family. It seems I'll always have feminine features, so they say. I really don't know what I look like other than a human being.

14. The Upstairs Maid

This is Frank, fabulous, fat, funny Frank, the spirit of Halloween.

Frank was such a gigantic hit on Halloween as The Upstairs Maid that he is making a career of it. He has appeared at parties, at gallery openings, and all kinds of special events. He has, in fact, become The Upstairs Maid.

It is truly amazing the way this big, corpulant man can carry off the role of so petite a character with such verve and flair. His secret is the genuine sweetness in his heart.

FRANK

Frank lives with his mother, Ada, who designed and made his costume and who accompanies him whenever he makes an appearance. Together they formed the real inspiration for this book. When Frank and "Mummsie" walked into the Halloween studio, everything stopped. Photographers and assistants crowded around while dozens of people lined up to have their pictures taken with The Upstairs Maid.

When we visited Frank and Ada in

their apartment, just off Polk Street, he greeted us in costume, daintily escorted us into a charming parlor, served us short-bread and tea, and overwhelmed us with a flood of photo albums, memorabilia, and recountings of bizarre episodes.

How did you come up with the French maid?

Well, it was two weeks before Halloween and several of my friends were going out, and they said, "We want you to go out this year," and I said, "Oh, what will I ever wear?"

I had a Shirley Temple costume which Mother made and which I had worn to a party, but I thought, you know, Halloween has to be a little more special, and then we saw a French maid's costume in a store, but it was a very straight-type dress, a uniform-looking kind of thing, and I said to Mother, "I want a little more flair, a little more flamboyancy, and I want a little lace, and, you know, I want it to look a little more chic," and I talked to my friends about it and they said, "Your size will just make it heaven. You've got to do it."

What exactly is your size?

I'm six feet tall and I weigh two hundred and twenty-five pounds. I told Mother

Frank: Mother always wanted a girl
and—and I said I was the girl she never
got, in true heart.

WHEN DID YOU CONFIDE TO YOUR MOTHER
THAT YOU WERE PERHAPS HER DAUGHTER
AND NOT HER SON?

Oh, dear, there used to be such a facade
on weekends. When I was in college,
I would always take my friends home on
weekends and I would, you know...it
was...we slept...we only had Mother's
bedroom and my father's bedroom and
my bedroom, which we shared, and so
forth. My friends, needless to say, were
very effeminate or hairdressers, or
whatever you'd say, and one weekend,
someone at college threatened to call my
parents and tell them I was gay, and I said,
"Well, there's no need to. I've already
confronted my parents with it." At the
time it was hard for them to accept. My
father, who died two years ago of a heart
attack, was a long-distance trucker, into
baseball and football and all kinds of very
macho, up-and-up stuff, and when I told
them, they thought...that whatever
happened in their genes...they thought
their child was the only gay child in the
entire world. My parents put me through
college and everything, and they said as
long as I never got into trouble that they
could accept that. They just couldn't
accept seeing their name on the front
page. Luckily I was never in trouble in our
home town, Williamsport, Pennsylvania,
a very small town with very bigoted
people.

TELL US ABOUT THE FIRST TIME YOU WENT
OUT IN DRAG?

The very first time I went out it was very
serious. I was escorted and everything
and...and a policeman invited me home!
He said, "I'd really like to take you home
and get it on with you," and I said, very
properly, quote unquote, "Well, I don't
think I have quite the right plumbing for
you," and he said, "You are a broad, aren't

what I wanted—I properly introduce
Mother as my designer—and she started
in on the sewing machine and came out
with this full, wonderful dress which took
eleven yards of material, and the apron
and the hat, the bows on the shoes, everything except the gloves, of course.

HOW LONG DID IT TAKE YOU TO MAKE THE
COSTUME, ADA?

Ada: Oh, I worked on it a whole week.
I used to buy dolls and dress them and
I had quite a nice little trade going with
them. I won first prize with my bride doll
and second prize for my bed doll at the fair
one year.

you?" and I said, "Of sorts, this evening," and he was very persistent so I said, "Well, are you into gay men?" and by this time he had lost about five smiles and his face turned into an Irish brogue of a policeman and he said, "Not really. I think they're justa buncha fags," so I said, "I don't think we'd get along." Those were fun years.

WHEN DID YOU COME TO SAN FRANCISCO?
I came here seven years ago and then, well, somebody came out here from Boston and talked me into moving there. Unfortunately he's a married man, so I moved to New York City. When my father died, Mummsie came to live with me there.

When I left San Francisco, I felt like Jeanette MacDonald, who left one time. I said to my friends, "I feel like I'll return as Jeanette MacDonald one day," and in fact that's my forte for next Halloween. I can do her trills. (*Frank breaks into song.*) San Francisco, open your Golden Gate!

AND YOU CAME BACK WHEN?
Just last year, with Mother. On the plane, just as we started circling the bay, tears were rolling down my face, and the stewardess asked, "Are you all right, sir?" and people looked, you know, thinking I was going to throw up, and I said, "I'm just fine. I'm home." And the next day Mother went downtown with me and marched in the Gay Parade all the way from the Ferry Building to the Civic Center with a sign that said, "I love my gay son." When Mother passes into her fairytale land, or whatever, and starts sewing for the angels of heaven, I'll have to get somebody to do my wardrobe.

Ada: All those wings will be hard to sew. I've retired. I won't sew in heaven, no, and I won't make suits for devils, either.

WHAT ARE YOUR PLANS FOR THE FUTURE?
I see myself in the future...I'd like to do some theater work. I sing and I'd like to do more fun things. I've done nine-to-five everyday business-type work. I've worked with people. I've worked as a sales clerk and had to put on the fake, million-dollar

smile for Christmas. For a long time I was a switchboard operator, or communications operator if you like, and, oh God, just got tired of it. I just wanted a different type of life. I wanted to do something I wanted to do for a change. I'd like to get into a more realistic way of living. I could free-lance as an upstairs maid. For a fee of twenty-five dollars—wouldn't it be fun?—think of me walking into the bedroom and serving your spouse, or whatever, breakfast in bed. I bring the rose for the tray. I do hope to find someone in my life who will accept a French maid. They have such vivid pasts, these upstairs French maids.

15. Wonder Woman

"Last call," said the bartender at Le Disque, throwing switches that turned off the disco music and turned up the house lights.

BOYD

Boyd, the cocktail waiter, quickly made his way from table to table, scooping up his tips and taking orders for one last desperate drink.

A few minutes later Boyd stood on the deserted sidewalk in front of the club with Sandra, his roommate, watching the desolate fog from Golden Gate Park waft down Haight Street. Sandra, still wearing her clown suit after a day of performing for tourists at Fisherman's Wharf, was explaining what happened to the car.

"They towed it away, Boyd. After all, it had eight hundred dollars worth of parking tickets. We'll have to walk home."

Boyd looked at her with terror in his eyes. "Walk home?... Across the park? Through *Mugger's Paradise?*"

"Don't worry. I'll protect you. It'll save us six blocks."

The park was deep in murk. Boyd

clung to Sandra as they stood at the edge of the shadowy grove known as Mugger's Paradise. During the day it was one of the most beautiful spots in the park, a stand of live oak and manzanita surrounding a secluded meadow, a favorite rendezvous of lovers and dreamers. But at night the manzanita rose up in grotesque forms, eerie shadows danced among the oak. Sandra hesitated a moment, then pushed on, Boyd clutching at her jacket.

Something moved in the bushes. "What was that?" they stammered simultaneously. Then something grabbed Sandra and she screeched, "Boooyyd..." and began to struggle. Frantically she looked around but Boyd had disappeared. She was being attacked by two teenage girls. One was pulling on her purse and the other was on the ground with her arms around her knees trying to knock her down.

Suddenly the scene was flooded with light. Out of the trees swooped a shining transparent aeroplane training a big spotlight on the assailants and their victim. The bad guys froze with fear. Sandra shrieked with delight. Wonder Woman strikes again!

So, muggers beware. Wonder Woman lives. In San Francisco, with an unsuspecting clown.

BOYD, TELL US WHY YOU BECAME WONDER WOMAN...

When I was a kid Wonder Woman was definitely my superhero, my favorite superhero, and I think, first of all because of the pure fact that she's an Amazon, and I've always had this attraction to Amazons for some strange reason. I don't know why. And because she flew around in a glass airplane, which I thought was a kick, as a kid.

When Sandra and I moved into this apartment two years ago, we decided to have a Halloween party with a superheroes theme. We thought that would be sort of a kinky thing. She asked me what kind of superhero I wanted to be and I said, "Wonder Woman, of course." Sandra made the costume, which cost like maybe thirteen dollars to make. It consists of a pair of white vinyl knee boots which I got where I work for seven dollars, a pair of navy blue dance pants with white stars sewn in one piece with a built-in bra. And I have large chest muscles so I just pinched my chest muscles more to make me look like I had boobs and I built the cleavage

up with makeup. The gold thing was just cut out and pinned on, the same with the bracelets. And a wig and a headband.

When this Halloween came, I said, "Gee, I never wore this out of the apartment last year. This year I'm really gonna do it." I shaved my body, put the outfit on, and hit the streets. I shaved my pits and my chest and I'll tell you, right there was enough. I'll never do it again,

never. It was wild! It was funny as much as it was painful, and itchy. Next year I'll go as a hairy woman.

TELL US ABOUT HALLOWEEN...
I really wanted to go as Diana Prince, Wonder Woman's cover-up identity, like Superman is Clark Kent, and halfway take it off and reveal the costume. I went out all day as Wonder Woman. I went down to the financial district as Wonder Woman for lunch with a friend, and people just couldn't believe it. Ha! Wonder Woman walks into a bank and cashes a check.

ARE YOU GOING TO DO WONDER WOMAN NEXT YEAR?
Uh-uh. Wonder Woman is put away in a little shoe box, and I don't think she'll ever come out of the closet again. She's hid away. Let Linda Carter do it.

WHAT'S NEXT?
I'd like to do Charo and Dinah Shore, and I'd like to do Queen Elizabeth, the queen now, 'cause I have an appreciation for natural tinted shoes and pillbox hats. This coming Halloween these two guys and I are planning to go as the Andrews Sisters, totally during wartime: the hairdos, military uniforms, and everything. We're rehearsing "The Boogie-Woogie Bugle Boy" and we're going to go around singing it.

CAN YOU SING?
Oh, no. I couldn't carry a tune if my head
was in a bucket, but I know the words.
Who's going to pay attention to my voice?
We're now arguing about who wants to be
Maxine, Laverne, or Shirley. Maybe after
that I'll go as the colonel or his chicken.
First of all, I don't think it's really chicken.
I think it's prefab hot dogs pressed around
old chicken bones. Oh, he's a strange one.
Would you like to see my Lieutenant
Uhura imitation? (*Lieutenant Uhura, a
lovely Swahili woman, is the communications
officer aboard the Starship* Enterprise *from
"Star Trek." Boyd sticks a salt shaker in his ear
and moves into the twenty-first century.*) "I've
tried all frequencies on warp five, Captain,
and still no response from the Klingon
vessel." How about Arlene Francis: "Are
you in show business? Are you animal,
vegetable, or mineral?"

ARE YOU NATURALLY SPEEDY?
Naturally, this is it. This is the way I am
all the time; well, not all the time, mainly,
yeah. I'm pretty hyper. There's a lot of fun
in this house. After all, Sandra's a clown
and I'm a klutz. She calls me a goon. I
guess I am a goon. Once I cooked this
whole spaghetti dinner and set it on a
table with a broken leg and the whole
thing went: Shoooooong! Everybody was
sitting around, you know, and Ecch! I
can't make spaghetti anyway. The reason
I'm so meticulous and everything is
because I'm a Virgo, and that definitely,
you know, nyarrroooow! Virgos are weird
people. Did you ever meet a virgin that
wasn't? I love frogs. If you look around,
there's frogs everywhere. That's my
favorite frog, Quaalude. And that's his
best friend, Benzedrine.

ARE YOU GAY OR BISEXUAL, BOYD?
Ah, shoot, it depends on the time of year.
I'm gay, okay? I don't dislike women, and
I'm not saying I can't have a love affair.
I've been married. Women are great, and
if the right woman came along, far out,
but I tend more toward men. I get turned
off by gay people who can't accept women
and can't accept straight people. It's the
same as straight people who can't accept
gays. I think that's sad, because there's a
lot to learn about other people. If everybody
had an open mind and accepted everybody
it would just be a lot better world. I have a
few gay women who are friends of mine,
and one woman says she would like to
murder every straight man on earth. I think
that's really stupid. That's not cool. I mean,
I accept those people, I just find them a little
hard to relate to. Now do you know why
I was Wonder Woman? Wonder Woman lives
everywhere. Don't you want to buy a
Wonder Woman mirror of your very own?
Come on, girl, buy it!